THE
SWEET
POLISH
KITCHEN

THE SWEET POLISH KITCHEN

80 recipes for celebratory cakes,
home bakes and nostalgic treats

REN BEHAN

PAVILION

For Ed, Edward, Elena
and Matthew x

INTRODUCTION

I make no secret of the fact that I have a sweet tooth, and I almost certainly inherited it from my maternal grandmother, Babcia Tekla. She was a resilient woman and would often share with me her memories of Poland. She had lived frugally and resourcefully, and was adept at making simple Polish dishes that always tasted heavenly to me.

My Babcia's speciality was *racuchy*, apple pancakes, made with apples from the garden, doused in a thick batter and fried until golden and crisp. To serve, she would dust them with a generous coating of icing sugar. I don't remember her being a technical baker so much, rather someone who enjoyed a sweet hit with as little fuss as possible. She made very good *placki*, potato pancakes, too, and I remember that she would sometimes add a grated apple (instead of onion), and serve them with a sprinkling of sugar and a good slurp of double cream, or sweetened sour cream, which she loved. The line between sweet and savoury was often blurred. There was balance, of course. '*Co za dużo, to niezdrowo*', Babcia would say, meaning, 'Everything in moderation'.

Everything I have learned about baking, I taught myself, or by watching others, or by talking to others. My Mama's approach was much the same; most things were measured by eye (*na oko*) or with a glass (a *szklanka*). Over the years, I've been given various bits of paper with scribbled-down recipes for Polish cakes and sweet treats. It's always hard to replicate the memories of generations passed, or even to match the memory of the perfect slice of cheesecake eaten in a Polish café. However, over the years, I have enjoyed baking and tinkering and perfecting some of my favourite recipes, as well as travelling to Poland in search of something new. This book, then, is as much of a resource for me as I hope it will become for you, and I hope that nothing is too complicated for you to have a go at. Some of the cakes and bakes might be a bit of a project, but what a lovely way to while away an afternoon. I have baked many of these cakes with my teenage daughter, Elena, and in turn, she has been inspired to create her own recipes. With an older brother, Edward, and younger brother, Matthew, on either side of her, we have had many willing helpers and taste testers.

Not everyone reading, baking or cooking from this book will have Polish heritage and you certainly don't need it. But if you do, then I hope that you enjoy some of the wistfulness and nostalgia here. Certainly, an appreciation of my Polish roots has fuelled me in writing this book and I can say, without hesitation, that those with Polish blood, even a drop, often feel the truest sense of connection through food.

There is also a beautiful Polish proverb that says, '*Gość w dom, Bóg w dom*', or, 'A guest in the home is God in the home', and I think this goes to the very heart of what it means to be Polish. It really means to be hospitable and to welcome people into your home with warmth and grace. You'll never leave hungry. There will always be tea and cake on the table, at least.

When I wrote my first book, *Wild Honey and Rye*, I wanted to do whatever I could to shine a light on the wonders of the Polish table. It has been a privilege and a joy to know of so many readers trying out recipes, and being inspired to venture into a Polish café or restaurant – or even to travel to Poland to experience Polish cuisine first-hand.

I hope that this collection of home-baked cakes and Polish sweet treats provides you with an even more delicious journey of exploration, adding a good dose of well-being and comfort to go with it.

Paternal Babcia Maria and Her Sister, Antonia

While writing this book, I came across a little story, in a book called *The History of the Marczak Family*, written by my cousin George Marczak. He documents the journey that my father Longin, his twin Jeremy, and their families took from Kresy, in the eastern borderlands of Poland to their eventual settled home in the United Kingdom. The twins were aged just sixteen when the Second World War broke out in September 1939 in Poland. They lived on settlers' land called Ulanska Dola, near Dubno, Targovice (now Ukraine), that had been given to my grandfather Stanisław as a result of his earlier efforts during the Polish-Bolshevik War. On 10 February 1940, the NKVD arrived in my father's village and began the process of deporting all of the soldier families. My grandmother Maria, and her sister Antonia, only had time to pack a few essential items. Whilst there, Antonia worked in a bakery, which had two sacks of dried grain in the store room. My father and his twin were given permission to go to the bakery, accompanied by guards, to collect the sacks for their journey to the Archangel region, or Arkhangelsk Oblast, Siberia, where they were forced to live in a labour camp. My grandmother worked in a *piekarnia*, a bakery, for

a while. They would save up what they had to bake bread, and then they would share it around other families in the camp. It was much later, in July 1941, when amnesty was granted to 388,000 Poles, that my father and his twin, and their father and my uncle Tadeusz, joined the Polish Armed Forces gathering in exile. In December 2022, the last of my father's family, my uncle Jurek, passed away. He lived to be almost one-hundred years old. He remembered the story of the two sacks of grain. They must have all been grateful for the skills of Maria and Antonia, who did what they could to keep the family fed. How lucky I am to have such heritage, and to have grown up with such heroic stories.

The Strands and Influences in Polish Baking

This book is a reflection of the many strands and influences weaving their way through the Polish kitchen and a collection of some of my favourite recipes. Historically, we know that Slavs settled in the territory known as Poland in the fifth and sixth centuries. Their diet was frugal and simple, and mostly made up of grains. Flours, *kasza* or groats would have been made from barley, wheat, rye and millet. There would have been wild fruits growing in the forests, perhaps bilberries, and honey would have been used to add sweetness. In terms of sweet treats, there is evidence of a sweet form of a flatbread, made with flour and water and sweetened with honey.

In around 966, Mieszko I, brought Christianity to Poland and it was during this time that fasting began, meaning that you could not eat meat, eggs or dairy. This is still observed in Poland in the period before Easter. The period preceding this being marked by *karnawał*, or carnival season, in much the same way as it is marked across the rest of Europe. Much later, life within the royal court, particularly during the reign of Queen Jadwiga, between 1373 and 1399, brought to the table luxury items and signs of wealth, such as imported spices (ginger, saffron and cinnamon), dried figs and raisins, sugar, honey, fruit and jams. We know that custard was eaten as far back as the Middle Ages.

The sixteenth century in Poland marked the Polish Golden Age, and welcomed Queen Bona Sforza d'Aragona, the Italian wife of King Zygmunt Stary, or Sigismund the Old. She was homesick for the food of her homeland and so brought chefs with her, who planted and tended to her royal gardens and who introduced citrus and other fruits to the table. The Polish Easter table, with a pretty basket, is often a focal point for sweet treats; *babka* cakes, for instance, have been present since the end of the seventeenth century. Gingerbread found its fame in Toruń, the birthplace of the famous astronomer Nicolaus Copernicus. The first mention of gingerbread was in 1380, although the earliest mention came before then, in 1293 in Lower Silesia. Made with flour, honey and spices, the Polish name *piernik* comes from the word 'peppery'. There are also links to a Slavic honey cake called *miodownik*.

Café culture thrived in Poland during the eighteenth century. The first café in Warsaw was said to have opened in 1724. After this, most of the cafés and pastry shops in Warsaw were opened by Italian, French, Swiss and German immigrants. At times, cafés were places used by people to plot uprisings and certainly people would use them as places to discuss politics and culture. During the war, many cafés and bakeries were destroyed. Indeed, even now, modern entrepreneurs are rebuilding and breathing new life into places lost.

Post-war and during communist times, the availability of ingredients was scarce and so the Poles, as they were used to, had to become even more resourceful. If they didn't have sour cream, they would use vinegar, salt, and baking soda. Far from taking a dip, some aspects of Polish food, including baking, flourished and cuisine became more creative.

Poland is the beating heart of Central Europe. A true crossroads between East and West. It is impossible to place every individual sweet treat or baked good into a particular time and place. But through taste and travel, exploration and curiosity, we open up a new world to discover – one filled with *szarlotka* and *sernik*, *babkas* and *bundts*.

POLISH
BAKING
BASICS

Throughout this book there are a variety of techniques, which I have tried to explain in a very straightforward way. There are recipes that are simpler to follow, and some that are more of a project, but as a home baker and not one who is professionally trained, I can say that all of these recipes are achievable. Added to this, I have a very keen thirteen-year-old baker at home, who has helped me test and fine-tune these recipes. And so, Elena and I hope that this encourages everyone, whether new to baking or not, to have a go.

A FEW TOP TIPS

- All eggs are large, unless stated otherwise.

- All butter is unsalted, unless stated otherwise.

- If not using fresh yeast, I use active dry yeast, and I usually add a tablespoon of flour, sugar and some liquid to get the yeast going. My recipes include the amount to use if using fresh yeast, or active dry yeast. Fast-action dried yeast or instant dried yeast, where specified, can go straight in with the dry ingredients.

- Where oil is required, I use sunflower oil or a light (not golden or unpressed) rapeseed oil.

- When using flour in sponge-cake recipes, the golden rule is don't overmix. Sift in the flour (usually the final stage) and then gently fold it into the batter until it is all incorporated.

- Prepare and measure all of your ingredients before baking. My daughter Elena taught me that if you have forgotten to take the butter out of the refrigerator to bring it to room temperature, you can place it on a plate and cover it with a hot bowl (pour some hot water into a bowl, then tip the water away and dry the bowl). This will bring your butter to room temperature without melting it. I once left a block of butter on a radiator to soften it – this did not end well.

- Baking with room-temperature ingredients (eggs, butter, cream, cream cheese) helps your ingredients to come together. Unless, of course, the recipe calls for 'cold butter'.

- This may sound obvious, but read through the ingredients list and all the steps of the recipe before starting, so that you have a sense of what you are aiming for. Grease and line your tins in advance of beginning a recipe. Always preheat your oven in advance of baking. Invest in an inexpensive oven thermometer if your oven is not 100% reliable.

- I bake my sponges and pastries in the centre of my oven and, while I give instructions for a fan oven, I use a conventional oven (with no fan). Ovens vary so much that I tend to give a baking bracket, such as 30–40 minutes. Baking requires you to watch and test: Look for a golden colour, but don't open the oven door too regularly. If, for instance, you are baking a loaf cake and you have achieved a deep golden colour, it is fine to open the oven door and cover it with foil for the remaining baking time. Make sure nothing catches or burns. Test with a skewer inserted into the middle of a cake – the skewer should always come out clean.

EQUIPMENT

BAKING TINS

At home I have a selection of baking tins:

My round cake tins tend to be spring form and measure either 20cm/8in or 23cm/9in across.

My rectangular tins measure 30 x 23cm/12 x 9in and 5cm/2in deep; they are usually called brownie tins.

My square tins measure 20 x 20cm/8 x 8in and 8cm/¼in deep.

MIXER

I have a stand mixer with a whisk attachment, a beater and a dough hook. Most recipes can be made with a hand-held whisk, and you can, of course, knead by hand. If you haven't got a stand mixer, put one on your Christmas list and it will open up a whole new world of ease and baking success. Alternatively, ask around – your local friends and neighbours might have one gathering dust in the cupboard.

MEASURING JUGS AND SCALES

This sounds obvious, but invest in a good measuring jug and an easy-to-read set of scales. In the Polish kitchen, recipes require *szklanki* or 'glasses', rather than cups, but I always find it's hard to guess the size. A *szklana* is usually 250ml of liquid. All of my Mama's recipes are measured in *szklanki*, so I have converted them into grams over the years, for greater precision. Likewise, old Polish recipes are measured in *dag*, which is a decagram. 1 dg = 10g. So, 25 dg flour = 250g of flour, and so on. This can be a little confusing, so I hope that this book serves as a good resource over old Polish recipes.

STOCKING YOUR POLISH PANTRY

The good news is that there are virtually no 'hard-to-find' ingredients needed to make any of the cakes, bakes or sweet treats in this book. Occasionally, I mention using potato flour, which seems to be more common in the Polish kitchen than anywhere else, but I also suggest alternatives, such as cornflour or arrowroot. Some recipes call for poppy seed paste or caramel – these can be bought in a Polish shop, or I have provided simple recipes for them in this chapter. Likewise, I use vanilla bean paste a lot in my baking, but don't let that stop you from splitting a real vanilla pod and scraping out the seeds. You can also make a batch of vanilla sugar or lemon sugar (see opposite) and experiment with those.

Here are a few Polish staples that I mention throughout, meaning that if you buy them and stock them in your pantry or refrigerator, you are more likely to have all the ingredients to hand to give some of these recipes a go.

CINNAMON – CYNAMON
Cinnamon is a common spice in the Polish kitchen – it goes into apple cakes, see pages 25 and 40.

CREAM CHEESE – TWARÓG
Cream cheese is a big feature throughout this book, but I don't want you to get hung up on getting the 'right' type of cheese. Normal supermarket cream cheese is perfectly fine for all of my recipes, and is – in fact – better than the most well-known 'branded' cream cheese, which tends to be a little sweeter. If you are at the Polish shop, you should look out for *twaróg sernikowy*, which is for cheesecakes in particular and which is already smooth, like normal cream cheese or curd cheese. You can usually buy a 1kg tub, which is helpful, as most cheesecake recipes here require a good amount of cheese. Other types of *twaróg* or white cheese tend to be too crumbly. If this is the type you have, then it is preferable to pass it through a sieve or to blitz it in a food processor until smooth. Full-fat is best.

FLOUR – MĄKA
- Wheat flour in Poland is *mąka pszenna*, but you can also buy a finer flour, or a sponge flour, called *mąka tortowa*. This is sometimes labelled as *typ 450*. Mostly, I use plain flour or self-raising flour.

- Bread flour, or strong white bread flour, is called *mąka chlebowa* or *typ 750* in Poland.

- Gluten-free flour is called *mąka bezglutenowa*. There are a few recipes that I often make with a gluten-free flour blend and I use it interchangeably.

- Potato flour is *mąka ziemniaczana* and I use that in my cheesecakes, but you can also substitute potato flour for cornflour.

HONEY – MIÓD

I always keep a jar or two of Polish honey in my pantry, as it goes into so many recipes and you can also add a spoonful to your yoghurt or semolina for breakfast. In my first book, *Wild Honey and Rye*, I gave instructions for how to infuse your own honey with herbs or elderflower. The Poles believe that honey is medicinal, and so a spoonful might be added to a hot toddy made with vodka for a cough. I like to keep a jar of wildflower honey, forest honey and buckwheat honey in the pantry for my recipes.

LEMON SUGAR – CUKIER CYTRYNOWY

You can make your own lemon sugar, or use a mixture of lemon and orange zest, and use it in most of the sponge recipes in this book, where a recipe calls for the zest of a lemon or an orange. In this case, simply use the required amount of sugar and leave out the zest. Use organic unwaxed lemons or oranges. If you start with granulated sugar and whizz it in a food processor, you should end up with the consistency of caster sugar, which I use most often in baking. Use 1 fresh lemon or 1 fresh orange to 250g of sugar. Wash your fruit and dry it, then use a vegetable peeler to pare the zest from the lemon or orange, taking care only to peel the very top part, not the white pith underneath, otherwise you'll get a bitter flavour. Put the sugar and the pared zest into a food processor and pulse until the zest breaks down into smaller pieces. Store in a jar and use within 1 week.

SEMOLINA – KASZA MANNA

Semolina is called *kasza manna* and I use fine semolina from the supermarket.

SOUR CREAM – KWAŚNA ŚMIETANA

I always keep this in the refrigerator for both sweet and savoury recipes. In sweet recipes, such as cheesecakes, I use an organic supermarket brand.

VANILLA – WANILIA

As mentioned, I like to buy vanilla bean paste, but a good-quality vanilla bean extract works, too. Alternatively, scrape the seeds from the inside of a vanilla pod.

To make your own vanilla sugar (which you can then use in any recipe that calls for both sugar and vanilla bean paste separately), use 500g of sugar and 2 vanilla pods. Cut the vanilla pods in half lengthways, then use a knife to scrape away the seeds. Put the sugar into a food processor, add the vanilla seeds and pulse, just until you see speckles of vanilla throughout the sugar. Transfer to a jar with a well-fitting lid and place the vanilla bean pods inside the sugar, too, as they will continue to release some aroma and flavour. Shake every now and again. Use within 3 months.

VINEGAR – OCET

Where my recipes call for vinegar, I like to use a fruit vinegar, such as a cherry vinegar or a plum vinegar. You can find these online, but look for a good-quality, artisan vinegar, made with fresh fruit.

BASIC RECIPES

MASA MAKOWA

Poppy Seed Paste

A few of my recipes require poppy seed paste, such as the **Seromakowiec** – Cheesecake with Poppy Seeds (page 118), or the Poppy Seed Cinnamon Buns (page 115). You can also buy this in a can from most Polish shops, but I often make my own and store it in the refrigerator. Note: you'll need a high-powered blender or a coffee grinder to grind the poppy seeds.

Makes about 500g

200g poppy seeds
160ml boiling water
150g mixed peel
100g raisins
50g plain flour
1 tsp baking powder
1 tbsp runny honey
1 tsp almond extract
40g butter, melted

Rinse the poppy seeds, drain them through a muslin cloth and then cover with the boiling water. Leave for 30 minutes.

Grind the soaked seeds in a high-powered blender or a coffee grinder. Set aside.

In a food processor, whizz up the mixed peel and raisins with the flour and baking powder. Add the honey, almond extract, poppy seeds and melted butter, and stir well.

Store in a sterilised jar in the refrigerator for up to 1 week. It also freezes well. Bring the paste back up to room temperature before using.

KRUSZONKA

Crumble Topping

Some recipes include a crumble topping, which is made by setting aside a little of the dough that you've already made for the base (for instance, see the *Szarlotka* cake on page 40). However, there are other recipes where a quick crumble topping is entirely optional, such as for the Wild Blueberry and Almond *Babka* Loaf on page 156. This is how to make a quick crumble topping.

Makes about 180g

50g cold butter
80g plain flour
50g caster or soft light
  brown sugar

Place the ingredients in a bowl and rub together with your fingers until the mixture resembles a crumble topping. Alternatively, you can whizz the ingredients together in a food processor.

PRAŻONE JABŁKA

Stewed Apples

When apples are in season (September/October for the Bramley tree in my garden), I always make a big batch of stewed apples and freeze them into separate containers. I use them for making the *Szarlotka* cake (page 40) or to fill the pancakes on page 128.

Makes about 900g

6 large Bramley or other cooking
  apples (about 1.5kg; peeled and
  cored weight 1.1kg)
juice of ½ lemon
200ml water
4 tsp soft light brown sugar
1 tsp ground cinnamon

Peel, core and finely slice or chop the apples into cubes, tossing the pieces in lemon juice as you work.

Transfer the apples to a large pan, pour in the water, sprinkle with the sugar and cinnamon, cover pan and cook over a low heat until they have softened.

Transfer to a clean, heatproof bowl and leave to cool. Use immediately or freeze until needed. Keep in the refrigerator for up to a week, or freezer for up to 3 months.

KREM BUDYNIOWY

Pastry Cream

This type of pastry cream, or custard cream, is used in the Napoleon or Papal Cream Cake (page 46), Carpathian Mountain Cake (page 93) and in the Doughnuts with Custard or Advocaat Cream (page 86). In Polish recipes, you'll often see an instruction for a packet of *krem budyniowy*, but if you can perfect a home-made version, you can use it in a variety of recipes, and you can also use it as a sponge-cake filling.

Makes about 600g

25g cornflour or potato flour
25g plain flour
4 egg yolks
150g caster sugar
1 tsp vanilla bean paste
250ml milk
250ml double cream
100g butter, at room temperature

Sift the cornflour (or potato flour) and plain flour into a bowl.

In a separate bowl, whisk the egg yolks with the sugar and vanilla, then stir in half of the milk and half of the cream. Pour this mixture into the flour in the bowl and whisk to a custard.

In a saucepan, gently heat the other half of the milk and cream, then add the custard mixture, stirring constantly over a low heat for at least 8–10 minutes. It is fine if bubbles form, but make sure it is heating very gently to avoid scrambling. The cream will thicken but keep stirring/whisking. You need to taste it at this stage – if you can still taste flour, keep it on the heat for a little longer and add a little more milk if it becomes too thick. You can increase the heat at this stage but keep whisking. It will continue to thicken once set. Once thick, take the pastry cream off the heat, transfer to a heatproof bowl and cover the surface with clingfilm so that a skin does not form.

When you are ready to use the pastry cream, make sure it is at room temperature. Tip it into a stand mixer, whisk, and then add the butter, bit by bit, until all the butter is incorporated. Chill again in the refrigerator until completely cold, until you are ready to use it.

MASA KRÓWKOWA

Caramel Sauce

Caramel sauce in Poland is sometimes called *masa krówkowa*, but it is also called *kajmak*. It is made from condensed milk and sugar. You can buy it in a can, either at the supermarket or in a Polish shop. Alternatively, you can make your own as follows.

Makes about 300g

200g granulated sugar
100g butter
150ml double cream

Put the sugar in a heavy-based saucepan and gently heat until it starts to caramelise and turn a golden/amber colour, no darker. Try not to stir it until the sugar starts to melt down and turn golden. As soon as the sugar has melted, take it off the heat, and use a wooden spoon to stir in the butter and mix vigorously. If the butter separates, just keep stirring for another 2–3 minutes. Finally, slowly pour in the cream and keep stirring until you have a smooth caramel sauce. Leave to cool, then transfer to a sterilised jar. You can keep this for up to 3 weeks in the refrigerator.

POLEWA CZEKOLADOWA

Chocolate Glaze

You can use this recipe to glaze your bundt cakes or the doughnuts on page 90.

Makes enough to glaze 1 bundt cake or 8 doughnuts

2 tbsp butter
100g good-quality dark chocolate, chopped
100g icing sugar
1 tbsp runny honey
2 tbsp boiling water

Melt the butter and chocolate in a pan, then stir through the icing sugar, honey and boiling water. Mix until smooth, then pour over your chosen recipe.

ŻAKWAS CHLEBOWY

Sourdough Starter

Making your own sourdough starter should not be too daunting, but it does require you to keep a little eye on it, and to feed it for a few days before it is ready. You can use either a strong white bread flour or an organic rye flour.

250–350g rye flour (preferably organic white rye)

50–100ml lukewarm water

1 large sterilised jar (about 800ml–1 litre capacity) with a loose-fitting lid

DAY 1
Mix 50g of the flour with the just lukewarm water – you want to form quite a thick paste. Stir and leave in a jar, loosely covered but not sealed, for 24 hours. If you don't have a lid, cover it with a cloth.

DAY 2
Mix another 50g of the flour with 50–100ml of just lukewarm water. Stir into the mixture from Day 1. Leave loosely covered for another 24 hours.

DAYS 3 AND 4
Stir the mixture and discard half of the starter, then repeat as above. You will have used 200g of flour in total by now. You should start to notice some bubbles coming to the top of the starter mixture.

DAY 5
Again, stir and discard half of the starter. Mix the final 50g of flour with 50–100ml of just lukewarm water, then stir into the starter and leave for a further 24 hours, loosely covered.

DAY 6
Your starter should now be very active, bubbly and it will have a strong smell. You can use this as a starter for your sourdough bread (see recipe on page 155) and it can be stored, covered with a tight-fitting lid. If it isn't active and bubbly, repeat the process of 'feeding' by discarding half the starter, then adding more fresh flour and water and leaving it at room temperature, loosely covered.

If you place your starter in the refrigerator, it will become dormant. When you want to use it, you'll have to refresh it. To do this, the day before you want to use it, stir and pour away half of the mixture. Add 100g of flour and 100ml of just lukewarm water and leave it at room temperature again for 24 hours, loosely covered.

POLISH CLASSICS

SERNIK

Classic Polish Cheesecake

This type of cheesecake, without a base (*bez spodu*), is also known as a *sernik Wiedeński*, or Viennese cheesecake, in Poland. It is said to have been brought to Poland by King Jan III Sobieski, after his victory in the Battle of Vienna in 1683. Since this is baked in a tin lined with baking paper and has no base, it is one of the easiest cheesecake recipes to have a go at. Polish cheesecakes rarely have a biscuit base in the way that American-style cheesecakes do, but rather have a pastry base. The Krakowians are said to have modified the Viennese cheesecake, by adding a pastry base and a lattice top, which became known in Poland as a Krakowian or royal cheesecake (a version of which you can find on page 36). I use a 20cm/8in tin for this recipe, but you could use a 23cm/9in tin, which will just produce a slightly shallower cheesecake. For best results, bake this cheesecake a day ahead and leave to chill in the refrigerator.

Variation: Stir through a handful of blueberries instead of the raisins.

Serves 10–12

200g caster sugar

200g butter, at room temperature

4 eggs

1 tsp vanilla bean paste

800g cream cheese or twaróg sernikowy (see Baking Basics, page 20)

200ml sour cream

150ml double cream

250g raisins

90g cornflour or potato flour

icing sugar, for dusting

Preheat your oven to 170°C/150°C Fan/Gas Mark 3½/340°F. Line a 20cm/8in round springform tin with a single sheet of baking paper. Push the paper into the tin, making sure that some of it sticks up over the rim – you don't have to do this too neatly. Wrap the outside of the tin with a large piece of foil.

In a stand mixer, beat together the caster sugar and butter for a few minutes until pale and creamy. Add the eggs and vanilla bean paste, and beat again. Add the cream cheese, sour cream and double cream, then beat until completely smooth. Coat the raisins in a little of the cornflour or potato flour, then stir them into the mixture along with the rest of the flour.

Pour the mixture into your lined cake tin, then tap the tin on the work surface to help settle any bubbles.

Prepare a bain marie: take a large, shallow roasting tin and fill it with hot water until three-quarters full. Place your cheesecake tin into the hot water and transfer to the oven. Bake in the centre of the oven for 55 minutes–1 hour. It is ready when the sides are firm but the centre is still a little jiggly. The top should be lightly golden. Once baked, turn your oven off, open the door slightly and leave the cheesecake inside the oven for 1 hour.

After this time, remove the cheesecake carefully from the oven and remove the foil from around the tin. Leave the cheesecake to cool down, then place it in the refrigerator to chill completely overnight.

The next day, carefully remove the cheesecake from the tin and remove the baking paper. Dust with icing sugar and cut into slices to serve.

KRAKOWIAN-STYLE CHEESECAKE

Krakowians are very proud of their traditional recipe for *sernik Krakowski*, also called a *sernik królewski* (which means 'fit for royalty'), likely based on the Viennese cheesecake brought to Poland by King Jan III Sobieski. This version is baked in a square tin, and has a shortcrust pastry base as well as a chequered pastry topping, giving it a special touch. It is also flavoured with candied peel, which adds to the effect of making it look as though it's studded with jewels. While a square tin is more traditional, this cheesecake can also be baked in a 23cm/9in round springform tin.

Serves 12

For the pastry base and top:

150g cold butter, diced, plus extra for greasing

300g plain flour, plus extra for dusting

1 tsp vanilla bean paste

80g icing sugar, plus extra for dusting

2 egg yolks; plus 1 egg, beaten, for glazing

For the filling:

4 eggs, whites and yolks separated

250g caster sugar

500g cream cheese, or twaróg sernikowy (see Baking Basics, page 20)

125g butter, at room temperature

1 tsp vanilla bean paste

45g cornflour or potato flour

grated zest of 1 orange

150g mixed, candied peel, plus extra to decorate

50g raisins

Put all the ingredients for the pastry (except the beaten egg for glazing) into a food processor and blitz until a dough starts to form. Tip onto a floured surface and bring together by hand. Roll into a ball, wrap in clingfilm and chill in the refrigerator for 30 minutes.

Meanwhile, preheat your oven to 170°C/150°C Fan/Gas Mark 3½/340°F. Grease and line a 20 x 20cm/8 x 8in square baking tin (about 8cm/¼in deep) with baking paper.

For the filling, beat the egg yolks with most of the caster sugar (reserve 1 tablespoon for beating in with the egg whites) until pale and fluffy. Add the cream cheese, butter and vanilla bean paste, and beat well. Stir through the flour, orange zest, candied peel and raisins.

In a separate bowl, whisk the egg whites with the reserved caster sugar until soft peaks form. Fold this into the cheesecake filling.

Take your ball of dough from the refrigerator and split it in half. Flour the work surface, then roll one half of the dough out to a rectangular shape to fit your tin. Don't worry if the pastry breaks up slightly, just use your fingers to press the dough into the base of the tin until it reaches the corners. Prick it all over with a fork and bake in the oven for 15 minutes. Leave to cool slightly.

Meanwhile, on a floured surface, roll out the remaining dough, then cut into thin strips with a knife or with a serrated pastry cutter.

Pour the cheesecake filling over the base in the tin, smooth it out, then place the strips of dough on top, first diagonally in one direction, then criss-cross in the opposite direction to form a lattice design. Brush the top of the pastry strips with the beaten egg. Bake for 45–50 minutes, then switch off the oven, leave the door slightly ajar and leave the cheesecake to cool inside for a further hour.

Transfer the cheesecake to the refrigerator and leave to chill overnight. To serve, remove the cheesecake from the tin, dust with icing sugar and decorate with some extra candied peel.

PEAR CRUMBLE CHEESECAKE BARS

For a variation on the classic Polish cheesecake, you can make this with canned pears or peaches. As pears go so well with chocolate, I like to make a chocolate base and crumble topping. The cheesecake filling is egg-free, and it also works if you use vegan cream cheese and a vegan crème fraîche in place of the cheese and sour cream, along with a vegan white chocolate. For the base and topping, you can use vegan butter or spread and leave out the egg (and do check that your cocoa powder is dairy-free).

Serves 8

For the base and crumble topping:

125g butter, plus extra for greasing

225g plain flour, plus extra for dusting

50g caster sugar

25g cocoa powder

1 egg

For the cheesecake mixture:

200g caster sugar

100g butter, at room temperature

1 tsp vanilla bean paste

750g cream cheese or twaróg sernikowy (see Baking Basics, page 20)

250ml sour cream

100g good-quality white chocolate, melted

45g cornflour or potato flour

1 x 400g can of pears or peaches, drained and chopped into cubes

Preheat your oven to 170°C/150°C Fan/Gas Mark 3½/340°F. Grease and line a 20 x 20cm/8 x 8in square baking tin.

Place all the ingredients for the base and topping into a food processor. Blitz until a dough forms, then tip this out and bring together loosely by hand to form into a ball. Split the dough in half. Wrap one half in clingfilm and put it in the freezer while you prepare the rest of the cheesecake.

On a floured board, roll out the other half of the dough until large enough to fit the tin. Press the dough into the tin until it reaches the edges, then prick the base with a fork and bake in the oven for 15 minutes. Take the base out of the oven and leave to cool.

For the cheesecake mixture, beat the sugar, butter and vanilla together in a stand mixer for a few minutes until pale and creamy. Tip in the cream cheese, sour cream and melted white chocolate, and beat until completely smooth. Stir in the cornflour or potato flour.

Pour the mixture over the base in the tin, then tap the tin on the work surface to help settle any bubbles. Scatter over the chopped pears or peaches. Take the dough out of the freezer and grate it, then sprinkle the grated dough over the top of the cheesecake.

Bake for 45–50 minutes, until the cocoa-crumble topping is crunchy and slightly darker in colour. If it starts to catch, you can cover the cheesecake with foil for the last ten minutes of baking. Switch off the oven, leave the door slightly ajar and leave the cheesecake to cool inside for 1 hour.

Chill overnight in the refrigerator for best results, then remove from the tin and cut into bars to serve.

LEMON AND POPPY SEED BUNDT

In Polish baking, a *babka* is a bundt cake, made in a fluted tin. The resulting cake is said to resemble the skirt of a grandmother (a *baba*, *babka* or *babcia*). It is often made with yeast, although this is a simpler sponge version made without it. There is a Jewish version of a *babka*, which is more like a plaited, yeasted loaf, filled with cinnamon jam. I explore more *babka* recipes in the Seasonal chapter (pages 105–125). Polish cooks will often use fine breadcrumbs, instead of flour, to coat the inside of the bundt tin. I use a 2.4 litre/10 cup bundt tin and decorate mine with lemon glaze, additional poppy seeds and edible flowers.

Serves 8

250g butter, very soft, plus 1 tbsp
    for the tin
250g self-raising flour, plus 1 tbsp
    for dusting
250g caster sugar
4 eggs, separated
1 tsp vanilla bean paste
grated zest and juice of ½ lemon
2 tbsp poppy seeds

For the icing:
juice of 1 lemon
250g icing sugar

To decorate:
1 tsp poppy seeds
edible flowers, such as dried
    cornflowers

Preheat your oven to 170°C/150°C Fan/Gas Mark 3½/340°F. Melt the tablespoon of butter and use a pastry brush to brush the insides of a 2.4 litre/10 cup bundt tin with it. Sift in the tablespoon of flour and shake the tin from side to side so that the flour sticks to the butter and coats the inside of the tin.

Beat the butter and sugar together until pale and creamy. Add the egg yolks, one by one, and keep beating. Add the vanilla bean paste, and the lemon zest and juice. Next, sift in the flour, and stir with a spoon until all the flour is incorporated. Stir through the poppy seeds. Finally, in a separate clean bowl, whisk the egg whites until stiff peaks form. Fold through the cake batter until all the whites are incorporated.

Pour the batter into your bundt tin and bake in the oven for 45 minutes, or until a skewer inserted into the middle of the cake comes out clean. Leave to cool in the tin for 15 minutes, then carefully turn out onto a wire rack and leave to cool completely.

To make the icing, mix the lemon juice into the icing sugar until a smooth paste forms. Pour this over the top of your bundt, sprinkle over some extra poppy seeds and a few edible flowers, and serve with lemon tea.

SZARLOTKA

Apple Cake with a Meringue and Crumble Topping

In present-day Poland, you will usually find a *szarlotka,* a type of apple cake, on every sweet counter and dessert menu, and there are many variations. Traditionally, the bottom layer of a *szarlotka* is made with pastry, making it more of a pie, although it can equally be described as a cake or dessert, with echoes of the French apple *charlotte russe* cake created by chef Marie-Antoine Carême in Paris in the eighteenth century. In Poland, an early recipe appeared in the nineteenth century in a popular cookbook by Lucyna Ćwierczakiewiczowa. She used stale rye bread as her base, although there is also a version called *szarlotka na kruchem cieście,* which is made with shortcrust pastry. There are a few stages to this apple pie, but it is hugely rewarding to make and if you have some pre-cooked or stewed apples in your freezer from a glut, then it is definitely worth making. In my previous book, *Wild Honey and Rye,* I shared the recipe for a classic tray-baked version, which is the one my Mama taught me. She presses two-thirds of the pastry into the tin for the base, and then freezes and grates the other third for the topping. This version is a little more decadent, with a layer of meringue. It has a tendency to 'puff up' and try to escape the tin, so you must chill it before attempting to release it.

Serves 8–10

For the pastry:

450g plain flour, plus extra for
   dusting

1 tsp baking powder

200g butter, at room temperature,
   cut into cubes

grated zest of 1 lemon

225g caster sugar

4 egg yolks (save the whites for the
   topping)

1 tbsp natural yogurt

1 tsp vanilla bean paste

For the filling:

6 large Bramley or other cooking
   apples, (about 1.5kg; peeled and
   cored weight 1.1kg; or cooked
   weight 900g)

juice of ½ lemon

200ml water

4 tsp soft light brown sugar

1 tsp ground cinnamon

For the meringue:

4 egg whites

a pinch of salt

300g caster sugar

2 tbsp cornflour or potato flour

icing sugar, for dusting

continued over-leaf

Grease and line a 23cm/9in round springform tin with baking paper.

For the pastry, place the flour, baking powder, butter, lemon zest and caster sugar into a food processor and blitz to a sandy texture (or use your fingers and bring everything together like a crumble in a bowl). Add the egg yolks, yogurt and vanilla, and pulse (or knead) until the mixture forms a dough.

Sprinkle a handful of flour onto a large board and tip the dough out onto it. Bring it together with your hands and roll into a ball. Divide the dough into one-third and two-third pieces, wrap both in clingfilm and place the larger one in the refrigerator and the smaller piece in the freezer until needed.

For the filling, peel, core and finely slice or chop the apples into cubes, tossing the pieces in lemon juice as you go. Transfer the apples to a large saucepan, pour in the water, sprinkle with the sugar and cinnamon, then cook over a low heat until they have softened. Transfer to a heatproof bowl and leave to cool. You could do this step ahead of time.

Preheat your oven to 180°C/160°C Fan/Gas Mark 4/350°F. Take the dough that is in the refrigerator and roll it out to a circle to fit the bottom of your lined tin. Alternatively, you can break the dough up into pieces and use the back of a spoon to push the dough into the tin. Prick the base with a fork, bake in the oven for 15 minutes, then remove from the oven.

Drain any liquid from the cooked apples (you can drink this) and spoon the apple filling over the baked base.

For the meringue, place the egg whites in a spotlessly clean bowl with a pinch of salt. Whisk, increasing the speed gradually, until soft peaks form. Keep increasing the speed gradually and tip in the sugar, little by little, beating after each addition. Once the meringue is thick and glossy, stir through the cornflour or potato flour, taking care not to knock out the air. Give it another quick whisk, then spoon the meringue over the apple layer in the tin and use a spoon to flatten it out.

Take the dough out of the freezer and grate it, then sprinkle over the meringue layer. Bake for 55 minutes until the top is golden, then remove from the oven and leave to cool completely in the tin.

To serve, carefully remove the cake from the tin, dust it with icing sugar and cut it into even slices.

WUZETKA

Chocolate Cream Sponge

The *wuzetka* cake originates from Warsaw, and it was said to have first been baked in a bakery along a road named the 'W-Z route' in Warsaw shortly after the Second World War (the road connected the eastern parts of the city to the western, the *Wschód-Zachód* areas, hence 'W-Z'). It is a classic chocolate sponge cake, baked in a square tin, filled with cream (the line in the middle of the road) and topped with a cherry. If you are baking this for adults or a party, you can add a little cherry vodka to your soak.

Serves 9

For the chocolate sponge:
120ml vegetable oil or mild, light olive oil, plus extra for greasing
200g soft light brown sugar
2 eggs
1 tsp vanilla bean extract
240g sour cream
200g self-raising flour
75g cocoa powder
1 tsp baking powder
1 tsp bicarbonate of soda
240ml freshly brewed/hot black tea

For the soak:
50ml cherry vodka 'Wiśniówka' or fruit tea

Optional jam layer:
250g cherry jam or plum jam

For the cream filling:
250g mascarpone cheese, at room temperature
800ml double cream
3 tbsp icing sugar

For the chocolate glaze:
2 tbsp butter
100g good-quality dark chocolate, chopped
100g icing sugar
1 tbsp runny honey
2 tbsp boiling water

To serve:
whipped cream for piping
fresh or canned, drained cherries

Preheat your oven to 180°C/160°C Fan/Gas Mark 4/350°F. Grease and line two 20 x 20cm/8 x 8in square baking tins with baking paper.

In a stand mixer, beat the oil and sugar until it starts to thicken. Add the eggs, one by one, and the vanilla bean extract. Stir in the sour cream. Next, sift in the self-raising flour, cocoa powder, baking powder and bicarbonate of soda and stir until there are no lumps. Finally, pour in the hot tea and mix again thoroughly.

Divide the batter evenly between the tins and tap them gently on a work surface. Bake for 30–35 minutes until an inserted skewer comes out clean. Cool slightly in the tins, then carefully turn out onto a wire rack and leave the sponges to cool completely.

To assemble, place one layer of sponge into the bottom of a lined tin and brush liberally with the soak. If using jam, spread a layer evenly over the soaked base.

For the cream filling, whisk the mascarpone, then add the cream and icing sugar and whisk until the mixture becomes firm. Spread the cream over the base and flatten slightly with a spatula. Place the second layer of sponge on top and place the tin in the refrigerator, ideally overnight.

When you are ready to serve, make the chocolate glaze by melting the glaze ingredients together in a non-stick pan over a medium heat until thick and glossy, then leave to cool slightly.

Remove the cake from the fridge and carefully take it out of the tin onto a serving plate. Pour the glaze over the top of the cake and smooth out. Cut the cake into squares. Serve with some piped cream and a cherry on top.

NAPOLEONKA

Napoleon or Papal Cream Cake

There are really two classic custard-cream-filled cakes in Poland: one is the *Napoleonka* or *kremówka*, and the other *karpatka*, named after the Carpathian mountains because of the slightly undulating layers that the choux pastry forms when baked. A *kremówka* is also known as *kremówka papieska*, or 'papal cream cake', as it was said to be the favourite of Pope John Paul II, who was born in Wadowice, where there is a really beautiful museum dedicated to his life. It was during a visit to his hometown that the Pope remembered a bakery in the market square where he and his friends would pool their funds together to buy a slice of *kremówka*. My mother-in-law's uncle Jurek used to go skiing with the Pope in the Tatra mountains of Poland, and I am sure they would have also enjoyed stopping for a slice of cake or two. It has certainly always been a favourite of mine. A *kremówka*, or *Napoleonka*, is made with thin slices of French pastry or puff pastry and filled with a thick custard cream. There is also a well-known Napoleon Cake, popular in Russia, made with lots of thin slices of puff pastry, so perhaps once you've had a go at a classic *Napoleonka*, you could try layering up more layers. For ease, I buy ready-made puff pastry and then the harder work goes into making the perfect pastry cream (*krem budyniowy*).

Serves 6

320g (or 1 sheet) puff pastry
(ready-made/ready-to-roll)
2 tsp milk
2 tsp caster sugar
icing sugar, for dusting

For the pastry cream:

2 tbsp cornflour or potato flour
2 tbsp plain flour
4 egg yolks
150g caster sugar
1 tsp vanilla bean paste
250ml milk
250ml double cream
100g butter, at room temperature

Make the pastry cream using method on p26, make sure it is at room temperature. Tip it into a stand mixer, whisk, and then add the butter, bit by bit, until all the butter is incorporated. Chill until you are ready to use it.

Preheat your oven to 200°C/180°C Fan/Gas Mark 6/400°F. Prepare your baking tray by lining with baking paper

Roll out your sheet of puff pastry and cut it in half lengthways, so you have two long slices. Place them on the lined baking tray. Prick with a fork, brush both sheets with the milk and sprinkle over the caster sugar. Bake in the oven for 10–15 minutes until golden. Remove from the oven and leave to cool on the baking tray.

To assemble the cake, spread the chilled pastry cream over one layer of the puff pastry. Top with the second layer of puff pastry and place back into the refrigerator for at least 2 hours before serving dusted with icing sugar.

DOUBLE PLUM CRUMBLE CAKE

I call this a double plum crumble cake, because during plum season, I like to use two different varieties of plum, normally stocked by my greengrocer, which are English Victoria plums and a second variety with a deeper purple colour and a yellower flesh, which are the closest variety to *śliwka węgierka*, a common purple plum most often used in Poland. It is absolutely delicious served with a drizzle of double cream, and it keeps really well in a tin for up to three days. Growing up, we had a beautiful plum tree in the garden, and it was always a treat when my Mama baked a plum cake.

Serves 8

750g plums (any variety, but try to get two different varieties, if possible – I like Victoria plums in season), stoned and sliced

For the cake:

240ml vegetable oil or mild, light olive oil, plus extra for greasing

225g soft light brown sugar

4 eggs

1 tsp vanilla bean paste

1 tsp grated lemon or orange zest

250g self-raising flour

1 tsp baking powder

For the crumble topping:

50g plain flour

50g butter, at room temperature

30g icing sugar or light soft brown sugar

Preheat your oven to 180°C/160°C Fan/Gas Mark 4/350°F. Grease and line a 23cm/9in round springform tin with baking paper.

Put the sugar and eggs into a stand mixer and beat for a few minutes until pale and fluffy. Slowly add the oil and keep beating gently, then add the vanilla bean paste and the lemon or orange zest, and beat again. Stir in the flour and baking powder, gently fold in, using a metal spoon, until all the flour is incorporated.

Pour half of the batter into your lined tin and scatter over half of the plums. Pour the rest of the batter over the top, then press in the rest of the plums.

Make the crumble mixture by rubbing together the flour, butter and sugar until you have a crumble consistency. Scatter this over the top of the batter.

Bake in the centre of the oven for 55 minutes, or until a skewer inserted into the middle of the cake comes out clean.

Leave the cake to cool in the tin before removing and serving. A drizzle of double cream goes really well over a slice of this cake.

DEEP-FILLED BILBERRY BUNS

These are a lovely project during berry season, and you'll find these in bakeries all over Poland in the summer months. Traditionally, they are made with bilberries, the wild, European cousin of blueberries, but smaller and darker in colour – although defrosted frozen blueberries or drained, canned blackcurrants will work well, too. They are called *jagodzianki*.

Makes 10

For the buns:

75g butter

60g fresh yeast, crumbled (or 20g fast-action dried yeast)

150g caster sugar

750g sponge flour, or plain flour, plus a little extra for dusting

125ml warm or tepid milk (see method)

3 eggs, beaten

1 tbsp vegetable oil

1 tsp vanilla bean paste

For the bilberry/blueberry filling:

250g fresh bilberries, washed and drained (or frozen blueberries, canned blackcurrants in syrup, drained)

3 tbsp caster sugar

3 tbsp fine, white breadcrumbs

For the kruszonka crumble topping:

50g cold butter

80g plain flour

50g caster sugar

1 egg, beaten, for glazing

1 tsp icing sugar, for dusting

For the buns, melt the butter and leave to cool. In a small jug, crumble in the fresh yeast, add 2 tablespoons of the sugar, 1 tablespoon of the flour and pour over the warm milk. Stir and leave to sit in a warm place for 15 minutes. The mixture will start to bubble. You can follow the same method if using fast-action dried yeast, but make sure the milk is just tepid, otherwise you will kill the yeast.

Take a large bowl, sift in the remaining flour, add the melted butter, the yeast mixture, the rest of the sugar, the eggs, oil and vanilla. Using your hands, work the mixture until a smooth, elastic dough forms. You can also use a stand mixer fitted with a dough hook for this part. Cover with a damp cloth and leave in a warm place for 1 hour.

Preheat your oven to 170°C/150°C Fan/Gas Mark 3½/340°F.

To make the filling, mix the fruit with the sugar and breadcrumbs.

For the crumble topping, place the ingredients in a bowl, and rub together with your fingers until the mixture resembles a crumble mix.

Line a baking tray with baking paper. Tip the dough onto a board lightly dusted with flour. Split the dough into 10 equal parts. Roll into individual balls and place each one on the baking tray. Cover with a clean, dry cloth and leave to rise for 15 minutes.

Flatten the balls slightly, then spoon 1 tablespoon of filling mixture onto each disc of dough. Form each into a ball around the filling, completely enclosing it. Return each bun to the lined baking tray, brush with a little egg wash and crumble over the crumble topping.

Bake in the oven for 25–30 minutes until the buns have risen and the crumble topping is golden. Serve while still warm, dusted with icing sugar.

YEASTED BUNS WITH SWEET CHEESE AND FRUIT

Sticking with the bun theme, *Drożdżówki* are sweet yeasted buns and they can be filled with a variety of fillings and formed in a variety of shapes. These are round buns, and if you press the centre down with a spoon, you can fill them with a little sweetened cream cheese (reminiscent of a cheesecake filling) and top them with fruit and a little crumble topping (*kruszonka*). *Drożdżówki* are also popular during carnival season in Poland, but I like to make them all year round.

Makes 6–8

For the buns:

50g butter

25g fresh yeast, crumbled (or 14g fast-action dried yeast)

75g caster sugar

300g plain flour, plus extra for dusting

125ml warm or tepid milk (see method)

1 egg, beaten

1 tbsp vegetable oil

For the sweet cheese filling:

200g cream cheese or twaróg sernikowy (see page 20)

1 egg

1 tsp vanilla bean paste

50g icing sugar

For the crumble topping:

50g cold butter

80g plain flour

50g caster or soft light brown sugar

To finish:

any fruit of your choice (soft fruits are best, such as berries, but you can also use stewed apples or chopped peaches – alternatively, use 1 tbsp jam)

1 egg, beaten, for glazing

1 tsp icing sugar, for dusting

For the buns, melt the butter and leave to cool. In a small jug, crumble in the fresh yeast, add 2 tablespoons of the sugar, 1 tablespoon of the flour and pour over the warm milk. Stir and leave to sit in a warm place for 15 minutes. The mixture will start to bubble. You can follow the same method if using fast-action dried yeast, but make sure the milk is just tepid, otherwise you will kill the yeast.

Take a large bowl, sift in the remaining flour, add the melted butter, the yeast mixture, the rest of the sugar, the egg and oil. Using your hands, work the mixture until a smooth, elastic dough forms. You can also use a stand mixer fitted with a dough hook for this part. Cover with a damp cloth and leave in a warm place for 1 hour.

For the sweet cheese filling, mix the cream cheese, egg, vanilla and icing sugar together until a smooth paste forms. Set aside.

For the crumble topping, place the ingredients into a bowl and rub together with your fingers until the mixture resembles a crumble mix.

Line a baking tray with baking paper. Tip the dough onto a board lightly dusted with flour. Split the dough into 6–8 equal parts, depending on the size of buns you would like to make. Roll into individual balls and place each one on the lined baking tray. Flatten them a little and cover with a damp cloth for 30 minutes.

Meanwhile, preheat your oven to 170°C/150°C Fan/Gas Mark 3½/340°F.

Take a large spoon and press a little 'dip' into the centre of each bun. Spoon in a little of the sweet cheese filling, top with a little fruit. Glaze the edges of the buns with the beaten egg, sprinkle with some of the crumble topping and bake in the oven for 25–30 minutes until the buns have risen and the crumble topping is golden.

Dust with icing sugar and serve warm.

MAZUREK

Lemon Cream Tart with White Chocolate and Rose Petals

It would be impossible to write a book on Polish sweet things without *mazurek*, a pastry synonymous with Poland and, in particular, with the Polish Easter table. There are so many variations that *mazurek* can, in fact, be enjoyed year-round. A *mazurek* is really just a tart, or a sheet cake, made with a short pastry base. The base should be shallow and flat with a little rim, like a picture frame. The topping, whether a lemon cream, colourful icing, chocolate icing or a caramel-fudge topping, becomes a blank canvas for decoration. You could use a hazelnut spread, at a push. At Eastertime, the *mazurek* will most often be decorated with nuts and dried fruit, depicting floral scenes and catkins, or pussy willow. Modern versions might be decorated with dried petals, or freeze-dried berries. The same can be said for the shape, be it rectangular, oval, round or square. I like to make mine in a fluted, rectangular tart mould, with a loose base (measuring 36 x 12cm/14 x 4½in), but you could also try making an oval shape, free-form. My go-to recipe is adapted from one of my oldest Polish recipe books called *Kuchnia Polska*.

Serves 8

For the pastry:

300g plain flour, plus extra for dusting

200g cold butter, plus extra for greasing

100g icing sugar

2 tbsp sour cream or natural yogurt

2 eggs, separated

1 tsp vanilla bean paste

For the filling:

2 eggs

grated zest of 1 lemon plus 80ml lemon juice

100g butter, cubed

100g good-quality white chocolate, chopped

To decorate (optional):

edible dried rose petals

good-quality white chocolate shavings

dried fruit and nuts

For the pastry, sift the flour into a bowl and add the butter. Rub together with your fingers until you have fine breadcrumbs, then add the icing sugar, sour cream or yogurt, egg yolks and vanilla, and bring the dough together. There is no need to knead. You can also make the pastry in a food processor, which is even easier. Wrap in clingfilm and leave your pastry in the refrigerator for 20–30 minutes.

If you are using a tart tin with sides, or fluted edges, lightly brush the tin with melted butter before using.

Dust a board with a little flour and roll out the pastry to about the thickness of a pound coin, or 3mm/⅛in, and carefully press the pastry into the tin and into the edges. If you are free-forming your pastry, leave a quarter of your pastry to make a rim, roll out your pastry and brush the edges with a little beaten egg white. Then, create strips with the remaining pastry and stick those around the edge to form a lip or a frame. Rest your pastry in the refrigerator for 30 minutes.

Preheat your oven to 200°C/180°C Fan/Gas Mark 6/400°F.

Prick the bottom of the tart with a fork and bake in the oven for 20 minutes, or until the base looks evenly cooked and golden.

For the filling, in a small pan, beat the eggs and add the lemon zest and juice. Gently heat over a very low heat, stirring all the time. Add the butter, bit by bit, until the mixture starts to thicken. While the mixture is warm, add the white chocolate and stir until smooth. Cool the lemon cream before filling the tart case.

Once filled, refrigerate your tart for at least 1 hour to set, then decorate as desired.

STONE FRUIT TRAYBAKE

This is a sheet cake or traybake recipe that I turn to time and time again, and it can be made with almost any stone fruit, such as plums or cherries, or even with apples or pears. I have also included an eggless, a gluten-free and a vegan variation, so there is really no excuse not to give this cake a go. Serve with a dusting of icing sugar and a sweet cup of lemon tea. You can find another of my favourite versions of this cake in my previous book, *Wild Honey and Rye*, made with seasonal plums and a sprinkle of poppy seeds, but this apricot version is equally lovely.

Serves 12

240ml vegetable oil, plus extra for
    greasing
225g caster sugar
4 eggs, lightly beaten
2 tbsp natural yogurt
1 tsp vanilla bean paste
1 tsp grated orange or lemon zest
250g self-raising flour
1 tsp baking powder
8–10 apricots (or other stone fruit,
    such as plums or greengages),
    halved and stoned
2 tsp icing sugar

Preheat your oven to 180°C/160°C Fan/Gas Mark 4/350°F. Grease and line a 30 x 23cm/12 x 9in baking tin with baking paper.

Put the caster sugar, beaten eggs, yogurt, oil and vanilla bean paste into a stand mixer. Beat for 5 minutes until pale and fluffy, then add the orange or lemon zest and beat again. Stir in the flour and baking powder, gently folding with a metal spoon, until all the flour is incorporated.

Pour the cake batter into the lined tin and gently press the halved fruit, cut-side up, into the batter. Bake for 55 minutes, or until a skewer inserted into the middle of the cake comes out clean. Leave the cake to cool in the tin.

Before serving, remove the cake from the tin and dust with icing sugar. The cake will keep well in a tin for up to 3 days.

Variations:

To make an eggless sponge, replace the eggs with natural yogurt by increasing the volume of yogurt to 250ml and add 1 mashed ripe banana. Alternatively, use 150ml of whipped aquafaba.

You can also make this vegan by using a vegan or dairy-free yogurt. Use 250ml, as above, and add 1 mashed ripe banana.

To make a gluten-free version, simply replace the self-raising flour and baking powder with a gluten-free self-raising flour blend of your choice. I like Dove's Farm gluten-free self-raising flour.

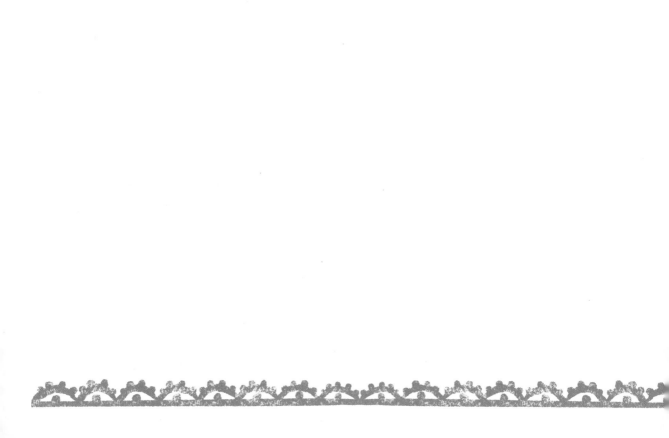

ŁAYER CAKES AND TRAYBAKES

STEFANKA

Chocolate and Honey Layer Cake

There are many cakes in Poland that are named after people. For instance, there is *tort Michałek* and *tort Mickiewicz*, named after the Polish poet, Adam Mickiewicz, whose epic poem, *Pan Tadeusz*, I studied at Polish A-Level. There's even one called *Pani Walewska*, after Mrs Walewska, thought to have been a mistress of Napoleon. My Mama used to tell me that when she was pregnant with me, she had an insatiable craving for *tort Stefania* (or *Stefanka*) – a Polish honey cake, covered in chocolate, named after some lucky lady called Stephanie. I like to think that this is where I got my 'sweet tooth' from. Traditionally, this cake also has a filling made with semolina, which is a useful alternative to making a crème pâtissière as it is easier to get the right consistency. A rectangular tin is best – I bake mine in two tins so that I have two even cake layers.

Serves 12

For the sponge:
a little butter, for greasing
6 eggs
200g caster sugar or icing sugar
125ml runny honey
300g self-raising or sponge flour
1 tsp baking powder
2 tbsp ground almonds
1 tsp vanilla bean paste or almond extract

For the semolina filling:
750ml milk
100g caster sugar
1 tsp vanilla bean paste
90g semolina
200g butter, at room temperature

For the honey soak:
2–3 tbsp runny honey mixed with 2–3 tbsp water

In addition:
1 x 300g jar of plum butter, plum jam or other fruit conserve

For the chocolate topping:
150g good-quality dark chocolate, chopped
100g butter, at room temperature
1 tbsp runny honey

continued over-leaf

Preheat your oven to 180°C/160°C Fan/Gas Mark 4/350°F. Grease and line two 30 x 23cm/ 12 x 9in rectangular baking tins with butter and baking paper.

In a stand mixer, with a whisk attachment, beat the eggs and sugar until pale and fluffy. This will take 10 minutes, so be patient. Add the honey and beat again. Sift in the flour and baking powder, and stir with a metal spoon until incorporated. Stir in the ground almonds and vanilla or almond extract.

Pour the batter equally into your cake tins, tap gently on the work surface to settle any bubbles, and bake for 15–20 minutes until golden and an inserted skewer comes out clean. Leave to cool in their tins.

Once cool, turn out the sponges and slice them evenly so that you have four thin layers of sponge.

For the semolina filling, gently bring the milk, sugar and vanilla to a rolling boil in a saucepan. Pour in the semolina and stir continuously until the mixture thickens. This will take at least 10 minutes on a low heat. Take care so that the mixture in the bottom of the pan does not burn. Tip the mixture into a heatproof bowl, cover with clingfilm, pressing it down on the semolina, and set aside to cool.

When the filling has cooled completely, beat the butter in a separate clean bowl until fluffy, then add the cooled semolina to the butter, a tablespoonful at a time, until it is all incorporated.

I prefer to assemble the cake in a rectangular tin lined with fresh baking paper. Place one layer of sponge into the tin and brush with a third of the honey soak. Next, spread a thin, even layer of plum butter/jam over the sponge, then spread a third of the semolina filling over the sponge. Repeat for the next two layers and leave the top layer plain.

For the chocolate topping, melt the chocolate, butter and honey together over a low heat until smooth and glossy. Leave to cool slightly, then pour the topping over the cake.

Leave the whole cake to cool in the refrigerator for 2–3 hours. When ready to serve, carefully remove the cake with the baking paper around it, then remove the paper before serving.

VANILLA AND ROSE CREAM CAKE WITH FRESH FRUIT, ALMONDS AND COCONUT

This is another delicious cake perfect for a party. The sides are decorated with almonds and coconut, and the cake is filled with fruit and cream. The sponge is made to a traditional Polish method, by whisking the egg whites and then adding in the egg yolks and sugar. This produces a light and airy cake, without any butter or oil. When you slice the cake, you'll see all the distinct layers of cream and jelly.

Serves 12

For the sponge:

a little butter, for greasing

8 eggs, separated

150g caster sugar

1 tsp vanilla bean paste or almond extract

200g self-raising flour

1 tsp baking powder

For the cream fillings:

750ml double cream

3 tbsp icing sugar

1 tsp vanilla bean paste

3 tbsp cocoa powder

For the rose syrup:

100g caster sugar

100ml water

2–3 drops of rose extract

For the jelly and to assemble:

2 x 135g packs of fruit jelly cubes

500g chopped fruit, plus any fruit to decorate the top

4 tbsp good-quality fruit jam of your choice (or use rose petal jam if you can find it)

150g finely flaked almonds

50g desiccated coconut

edible fresh rose petals, to decorate

continued over-leaf

Make up the jelly according to the packet instructions, but using 850ml/1½ pints of liquid. Using a rectangular baking tin, wet the tin slightly, then pour in the jelly liquid. Scatter in the chopped fruit so it is evenly distributed in the jelly. Place this in the refrigerator, ideally overnight, to set completely.

Preheat your oven to 180°C/160°C Fan/Gas Mark 4/350°F. Grease and line a 30 x 23cm/12 x 9in baking tin, at least 5cm/2 in deep, with butter and baking paper.

In a spotlessly clean bowl, whisk the egg whites until they form stiff peaks. Slowly add the sugar and keep whisking for 2–3 minutes, then add the egg yolks, one by one, and whisk until incorporated. Add the vanilla or almond extract, sift in the flour and the baking powder, and gently fold through until fully incorporated.

Pour the batter into the tin and bake in the centre of the oven for 30 minutes, trying not to open the door. After 30 minutes, check that the cake is cooked through. It will be fully cooked when an inserted skewer comes out completely clean. Leave the cake to cool in the tin. Once cool, carefully take the cake out. You can do this ahead and leave it to cool in the tin overnight, or in the refrigerator.

To make the cream fillings, whip the double cream with the icing sugar and vanilla until thick. Place half of the mixture into a separate bowl and stir the cocoa powder through that half.

To make the rose syrup, simply boil the sugar, water and rose extract together in a small saucepan over a medium heat until the sugar has dissolved. Leave to cool slightly before using.

Once completely cool, slice the cake into three even layers. Line the same rectangular cake tin with clingfilm so that the clingfilm hangs over the edges. Place the bottom layer of sponge into the tin and brush over half of the rose syrup soak. Spread the jam over the sponge, then spread over half of the chocolate cream filling.

Place the middle layer of sponge on top. Brush over the remaining rose syrup. For the jelly layer, remove the set jelly from the refrigerator. Quickly dip the jelly tin in boiling water which will help to release the jelly cleanly. Carefully, place your set jelly layer on the middle layer of sponge and then place the third piece of sponge on top.

Spread over the vanilla cream filling. Return to the refrigerator to set for 30 minutes. Place the remaining chocolate cream filling in the refrigerator to chill. When the cream layer has firmed up, remove the cake from the tin and discard the clingfilm.

Spread the remaining chocolate cream filling around the sides of the cake and smooth using a palette knife.

Gently toast the almonds and coconut in a frying pan over a medium heat until golden, shaking the pan often and taking care that the coconut doesn't catch. Cool, then press the almonds and coconut into the sides of the cake. Decorate the top with fruit and rose petals and chill for a final 1–2 hours before serving.

CARAMELISED PEAR AND CHOCOLATE CAKE WITH GANACHE

GF

For times when only a chocolate cake will do. I like to use E. Wedel chocolate, not least because it gives me an excuse to go to the *Pijalnia Czekolady* – a well-known drinking-chocolate café when in Poland. Karol Wedel established a chocolate shop and craft workshop on Miodowa Street in Warsaw in 1851. Karol and his wife served drinking chocolate, as well as other treats, passing their business over to their son Emil in 1865. Emil had practised his confectionery skills earlier in Paris. My favourite chocolate is their milk chocolate, or *czekolada mleczna*. You can widely find this online or in Polish delis. This cake is layered with caramelised pears, but if you can find them, you could roast some quince for extra decadence. The Poles also make a lovely quince vodka, called *pigwowa*, which is a golden colour and made with pears and apple. If you can find that, it makes a wonderful soak. Decorate this cake with some dried pears, or physalis. You can use normal sponge flour if you don't need to make a gluten-free version.

Serves 8

For the chocolate cake:

a little butter, for greasing

125ml milk (or use almond milk)

1 tbsp espresso powder mixed with 60ml hot water

1 tsp vanilla bean extract

300g soft light brown sugar

3 eggs

60ml vegetable oil or mild, light olive oil (or use 85g melted butter)

300g gluten-free self-raising flour (or self-raising sponge flour)

2 tsp gluten-free baking powder

a pinch of sea salt

125ml sour cream or buttermilk

100g good-quality dark chocolate, melted

For the caramelised pears:

1 tbsp butter

3 medium pears, peeled, halved and cored

80g soft light brown sugar

1 tbsp water

For the chocolate ganache:

150ml double cream

150g good-quality milk chocolate, such as E. Wedel classic milk chocolate, chopped

For the soak:

100ml pear syrup or pear juice; or quince vodka mixed with a little water and 1 tsp caster sugar

To decorate:

dried pear slices, or physalis fruit with leaves

Preheat your oven to 180°C/160°C Fan/Gas Mark 4/350°F. Grease and line two 23cm/9in round cake tins with butter and baking paper.

Gently warm the milk and add the coffee and vanilla. Leave to cool.

In a stand mixer, beat the sugar and eggs until pale and fluffy. Slowly pour in the oil (or melted butter). Sift in the flour, baking powder and salt. Pour in the coffee and milk mixture, then stir in the sour cream or buttermilk. Finally, pour in the melted chocolate and mix together well.

Divide the mixture equally between your prepared tins. Bake in the centre of the oven for 30 minutes, or until an inserted skewer comes out clean. Leave to cool in the tins for 10 minutes, then turn out onto to a wire rack and leave to cool completely.

For the caramelised pears, melt the butter in a frying pan over a medium heat. Place the pear halves into the pan until you get a little colour on the flat sides, then flip them over. Add the sugar and water to the pan and cook gently for 3–4 minutes until a caramel forms and the pears start to soften. Coat the pears with the sauce and leave to cool. Once cool, chop into cubes.

For the ganache, heat the cream gently in a pan. Add the chocolate and whisk until melted. Remove from the heat and keep whisking for 2 minutes. Leave the ganache to cool a little, then whisk again before using.

Neaten up your sponges by cutting around the edges and flattening any domed tops. Place one of the sponges onto a cake stand or a plate and drizzle over half of the soak. Scatter over the caramelised pears, then pour over half of the ganache and spread it out a little until it just touches the edges. Brush the underside of your second sponge with the rest of the soak, then place it soak-side down onto the pears. Pour over the remaining ganache and decorate as you wish.

LAYERED BIRTHDAY CREAM TORTE

This is a classic Polish birthday or celebration cake made with fresh cream and fruit. You can make it boozy by using a fruit liqueur or flavoured vodka as your soak. Feel free to experiment with a gluten-free flour blend. For a more modern version, you can leave the sides naked, but for a more classic torte, you should make double the amount of the vanilla cream and spread it around the sides. Pipe a few rosettes on top, if you wish.

Serves 12

For the sponge:

butter, for greasing

225g caster sugar

4 eggs

2 tbsp natural yogurt

1 tsp vanilla bean paste

250ml vegetable or sunflower oil

250g self-raising flour (or try a gluten-free blend)

1 tsp baking powder

grated zest of ½ lemon

For the honey-roasted strawberries (optional):

500g strawberries, hulled and halved

1 tbsp caster sugar

1–2 tbsp water

a drizzle of runny honey

For the vanilla cream:

500ml double cream

1 tbsp icing sugar

1 tsp vanilla bean paste

250g mascarpone cheese, at room temperature

To finish:

100ml soaking liquid (optional – if not using roasted strawberries), e.g liqueur or syrup from a can of cherries

8 tbsp good-quality fruit jam of your choice (optional – if not using roasted strawberries)

500g raspberries or chopped strawberries for the cream layers, plus fruit to decorate the top (optional)

2 tbsp caster sugar (optional)

50g walnuts or hazelnuts, finely chopped

continued over-leaf

Preheat your oven to 180°C/160°C Fan/Gas Mark 4/350°F. Grease and line a 20cm/8in round springform or loose-based cake tin, that is at least 10cm/4in deep, with butter and baking paper.

For the sponge, beat together the sugar and eggs in a stand mixer until pale and fluffy. Add the yogurt, vanilla and oil, then beat again for a minute or two. Sift in the flour and baking powder, add the lemon zest, then fold together until there are no lumps. Pour the batter into your prepared tin and bake in the centre of the oven for 40–50 minutes, or until a skewer inserted into the middle of the cake comes out completely clean. Leave the cake to cool in the tin (you can do this ahead of time and leave overnight, or in the refrigerator, if you wish).

While the oven is on, if you are making roasted strawberries, place the strawberries on a lined baking tray, sprinkle over the sugar and drizzle over the water (this will form a syrup). Roast for 10 minutes, then drizzle with the honey and roast again for a further minute. Remove from the oven and strain the syrup from the softened strawberries into a bowl. In a separate bowl, purée the strawberries slightly or mash with a fork.

For the vanilla cream, whip the cream for 3–4 minutes until just thickened. Be careful not to overwhip. Add the sugar, vanilla and mascarponè, and whisk until a smooth mixture forms.

Once cool, carefully remove the cake from the tin and carefully slice it into three even layers.

To assemble, wash and clean the cake tin and line with clingfilm – use a large enough piece to fold the excess over the top once assembled. Alternatively, you can make a collar for the cake using a piece of acetate, or a double-lined piece of baking paper to fit the tin. Take one sponge layer and place it in the bottom of the tin. If using, drizzle over some of the strawberry syrup and scatter over some of the mashed or puréed strawberries. (Alternatively, use some liqueur or syrup from canned fruit as your soak and a good-quality jam – brush with 50ml of the soaking liquid and spread over half of the jam.) Top with half of the fruit, then top with a third of the vanilla cream, spreading it into an even layer with a spatula. (If your fruit is not quite sweet enough, sprinkle 1 tablespoon of caster sugar over each layer.) Repeat this process with the next layer of sponge. Top with the final layer of sponge and spread over the remaining vanilla cream. Carefully wrap the cake with the excess clingfilm and chill in the refrigerator for at least two hours.

Once chilled, take the cake out of the tin and remove the clingfilm. Decorate the top of your cake with the chopped nuts and fresh fruit (if using) and keep chilled until serving.

'NO-BAKE' COCONUT AND ALMOND CAKE

The art of the 'no-bake' cake is worth learning and pulling off once in a while. Poles very often use *herbatniki*, which are tea biscuits, as a shortcut in layer cakes and the variations are endless. Alternatively, as in the Layered Raspberry and Lemon Cloud Cake (page 70), they use trifle sponge fingers. This recipe is inspired by the flavours of a Rafaello chocolate, which is a coconut-almond truffle that you can find anywhere. It won't win you any awards in the *Bake Off* tent for the crumb or for authenticity, but it's a satisfying and tasty cheat. For the biscuits, rich tea fingers work best, or you could try French-style Petit Beurre biscuits. While you might think that 'no-bakes' are a modern social media phenomenon, there were, in fact, many wafer cakes adapted by Poles, not least, the *tort Pizingera*, a Viennese cake made with Pischinger wafer biscuits.

Serves 9

For the filling:

600g cream cheese, or twaróg sernikowy *(see page 20)*

200ml double cream

100g caster sugar

1 tsp almond extract

100g desiccated coconut, toasted lightly in a pan and cooled

To assemble:

200g rich tea finger biscuits

200ml double cream

1 tbsp icing sugar

100g good-quality white chocolate, chopped

20g blanched almonds, chopped

Line a 20cm/8in square baking tin with baking paper.

Make the filling by mixing together the cream cheese, cream, caster sugar and almond extract until smooth. Stir in the toasted desiccated coconut.

Line the bottom of the tin with a single layer of rich tea biscuits. Spoon over some of the filling, then repeat to make three layers in total. Place a final layer of rich tea biscuits on the top. Whip the cream with the icing sugar until slightly thickened, spread it over the top of the 'cake', then place in the refrigerator to chill.

Once chilled, melt the white chocolate and stir in the chopped almonds. Pour this mixture over the top of the 'cake', allow the chocolate to cool a little, then serve.

LAYERED RASPBERRY AND LEMON CLOUD CAKE

This is often called a *malinowa chmurka* or 'raspberry cloud'. It is a layered cake made with sponge and raspberry jelly, but you can also use strawberry jelly or experiment with other flavours. It's fun to make and I like to rope in some small helpers, to assist with the fruit and jelly and the building of the cake. The jelly layer and the meringue layer can be made in advance. For a simpler version, you can leave out the meringue layer and simply top with lightly whipped cream – you'll still get the cloud effect. It's a big cake and great for a party!

Serves 12

2 x 135g packs of raspberry jelly cubes
500g raspberries (or any kind of fruit)
4 tbsp lemon curd
icing sugar, for dusting

For the sponge:
butter, for greasing
225g caster sugar
4 eggs
2 tbsp natural yogurt or sour cream
1 tsp vanilla bean paste
250ml vegetable or sunflower oil
250g self-raising flour (or try a gluten-free blend)
1 tsp baking powder
grated zest of ½ lemon

For the meringue topping:
4 egg whites
120g caster sugar
120g icing sugar
2 tsp cornflour

For the cream layer:
500ml double cream
250g mascarpone cheese
50g icing sugar
1 tsp vanilla bean paste
1 tsp grated lemon zest
1 tbsp lemon curd

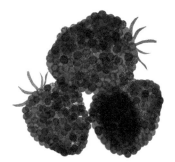

Make up the jelly according to the packet instructions, but using 850ml/1½ pints of liquid. Using a 30 x 23cm/12 x 9in rectangular baking tin, wet the tin slightly, then pour in the jelly liquid. Sprinkle in the fresh raspberries so they are evenly spread in the jelly. Place this in the refrigerator, ideally overnight, to set completely.

Preheat your oven to 180°C/160°C Fan/Gas Mark 4/350°F. Grease and line a second deep 30 x 23cm/12 x 9in rectangular baking tin with butter and baking paper.

For the sponge, whisk together the sugar and eggs in a stand mixer until pale and fluffy. Beat in the yogurt, vanilla and oil for 1–2 minutes, then sift in the flour and baking powder. Add the lemon zest, then fold together until there are no lumps.

Pour the batter into your prepared tin and tap it on the work surface to remove any air bubbles. Bake in the centre of the oven for 25–30 minutes, or until an inserted skewer comes out completely clean. Remove the cake from the tin and leave to cool completely, or chill in the refrigerator.

Cut your sponge in half so that you have two thin layers. Re-line the tin with a sheet of baking paper that overhangs slightly to make it easier to remove the finished cake. Place one layer of sponge into the bottom of the tin, spread the lemon curd over the sponge. For the jelly layer, remove the set jelly from the refrigerator. Quickly dip the jelly tin in boiling water which will help to release the jelly cleanly.

Carefully place your set jelly layer on top of the sponge, then place the second layer of sponge on top. Place the cake in the refrigerator to chill.

Next, make the meringue. Preheat your oven to 140°C/120°C Fan/Gas Mark 1/275°F. Take another 30 x 23cm/12 x 9in baking tin and line it with baking paper. In a spotlessly clean bowl or in a stand mixer, whisk the egg whites until they start to thicken, then add the caster sugar and beat again for 3–4 minutes. Sift in the icing sugar and cornflour, then fold in until incorporated, taking care not to knock out the air. Tip this mixture into your lined tin and spread out, so that it isn't quite smooth but has some peaks. Bake in the oven for 1 hour–1 hour 10 minutes. Remove from the oven and leave to cool in the tin.

For the cream layer, whip the double cream until it is just starting to thicken. Add the mascarpone, icing sugar, vanilla, lemon zest and lemon curd, and whisk again until just thick. Don't overwhip the cream. You want it to hold, but you don't want it to thicken like butter.

Take your cake out of the refrigerator, remove it from the tin and place on a large platter. You can trim the edges of the cake with a sharp knife to neaten it up a bit. Cover the top of the cake with the whipped cream mixture. Sit the meringue layer on top. Finally, dust it all over with plenty of icing sugar.

If you are not going to serve the cake straight away, leave the meringue in an airtight tin and place the rest of the cake in the refrigerator until you are ready to serve. Add the meringue layer just before serving.

MARCZELLO

Chocolate, Hazelnut and Cherry Torte

Recently, a friend in a group called 'Manchester Poles Reunited' posted a vintage menu from a New Year's Eve celebration, *Bal Sylwestrowy*, in Sopot, from 1958. On the menu was a spectacular-sounding cake called a *Tort Marczello*, which I had to research immediately. I found various incarnations, and the closest was one called a Marcello Cake, all of which pointed to a multi-layered chocolate and cherry sponge. So, this is my version. I like the fact that the Polish version takes half of my maiden name, Marczak. Make it for New Year, or at any time you fancy a show-stopping chocolate number. A little patience is required, as you will achieve a better result by baking each layer separately.

Serves 8–10

For the sponge:

9 eggs

200g caster sugar

100ml vegetable oil or mild, light olive oil

1 tsp vanilla bean paste

200g gluten-free self-raising sponge flour

100g cocoa powder

2 tsp gluten-free baking powder

For the pastry cream:

5 eggs

200g caster sugar

250g butter, chopped into cubes

50g chocolate hazelnut spread

100g cocoa powder

For the soak and assembly:

100g drained cherries (canned or preserved in kirsch), plus about 200ml liquor from the can or jar

To decorate (optional):

200ml double cream, whipped, for piping

2 tbsp icing sugar

a few fresh cherries, pitted

a handful of chopped hazelnuts

continued over-leaf

Preheat your oven to 180°C/160°C Fan/Gas Mark 4/350°F.

For the sponge, beat the eggs with the caster sugar in a stand mixer until thick, pale and fluffy. Slowly pour in the oil, keep beating and add the vanilla. Sift in the flour, cocoa and baking powder, and fold in with a metal spoon.

Line two rectangular baking trays with baking paper. Draw a circle on each using a 23cm/9in round cake tin as a stencil. Spoon or pipe about 5 tablespoons of the sponge batter onto each circle so that you have a thin layer of batter. Bake for 8 minutes until set, then tip out onto a wire rack to cool. Repeat this process (with much patience) until you have used up all of the sponge batter – you should have 8 even layers.

For the pastry cream, create a bain marie: place a small pan on the hob and fill it with a 5cm/2in depth of boiling water, then place a large heatproof bowl over the top of the pan, but ensure the water doesn't touch the base of the bowl. Add the eggs and sugar to the bowl and begin whisking. Over time, this mixture will become thick and fluffy. Keep the temperature of the boiling water low. Once the mixture is thick and creamy, take it off the heat and leave it to cool completely. Once cooled, place the mixture into the bowl of a stand mixer and begin to beat. Add the butter, in cubes, bit by bit, and beat until the butter is fully incorporated. Next, stir in

the chocolate hazelnut spread, then sift in the cocoa powder and fold it through. Leave the pastry cream in the refrigerator, covered with clingfilm, until you are ready to assemble your cake.

Line the same round cake tin (used as a stencil earlier) with clingfilm and assemble the cake inside the tin. Taking one layer of cake at a time, brush a little of the liquor for the soak onto the sponge, then add a thin layer of the pastry cream, smoothing it out completely. You can sprinkle a few of the canned or preserved cherries on each layer. Repeat with all of the sponge layers, pressing each layer down gently with the palm of your hand as you add the pastry cream. Once you get to the top, leave it plain and place something a little heavy (such as a side plate) on the top to weigh the cake down. Chill in the refrigerator overnight. Keep the remaining pastry cream in the refrigerator, too.

When you are ready to serve the cake, gently remove it from the tin and peel away the clingfilm. Place it on a cake stand, as it will be difficult to transfer it once it is decorated. Spread the remaining pastry cream over the top. For a retro feel (as with the *Wuzetka* cake, page 44), whip the double cream with the icing sugar and use it to pipe some cream rosettes on top of the cake, then top each rosette with a fresh cherry. Or, scatter over the chopped hazelnuts.

PLUM CRUMBLE TART

This is a simple plum tart, usually made with Polish plums called *śliwki węgierki*, or common purple plums (although any variety works; for instance, Victoria plums in season in England). The plums are roasted with sugar and honey before the crumble topping goes on. A scoop of vanilla ice cream works well to serve.

Serves 9

For the pastry:

100g cold butter, cubed, plus extra
    for greasing

150g plain flour, plus extra for
    dusting

50g icing sugar

2 tbsp sour cream or natural
    yogurt

1 egg yolk

1 tsp vanilla bean paste

For the crumble topping:

50g plain flour

50g butter, at room temperature

50g soft light brown sugar

50g ground almonds

To finish:

500g fresh plums (or 5–6 plums)

2 tbsp soft light brown sugar

icing sugar, for dusting

Preheat your oven to 180°C/160°C Fan/Gas Mark 4/350°F. Grease and line a 23cm/9in square baking tin with baking paper.

Put all the pastry ingredients into a food processor and blitz until they come together. Tip the pastry onto a floured surface and bring it together by hand. Knead for 2 minutes, or until the dough comes together smoothly. Wrap in clingfilm and chill in the refrigerator for 20 minutes.

For the crumble topping, put all the ingredients into a large bowl. Using your fingers, rub the ingredients together until you get a crumble-like mixture. Set aside.

Take out your pastry, lightly sprinkle some flour over a board and roll out the pastry to the size of the tin. Press the pastry into the bottom of the tin, prick it gently with a fork and bake in the oven for 15 minutes. Remove from the oven.

De-stone the plums and slice them thinly. Arrange the plums over the pastry and sprinkle over the sugar. Bake for 15–20 minutes to soften the plums. Check on them after 15 minutes – you want them to be soft and with a little juice starting to ooze out. Remove from the oven and sprinkle over the crumble topping, then bake for a further 15 minutes until the top is golden.

Leave to cool in the tin, then remove, cut into squares and sprinkle with a little icing sugar to serve.

SOUR CREAM ALMOND APPLE CAKE

This is a rustic apple cake made with almonds and you could easily use a gluten-free flour blend to make this a gluten-free cake. This was a favourite of my grandmother, Babcia Tekla, who always had an abundance of apples in her garden, and would either make a simple cake like this one or apple pancakes, depending on her mood. The ground almonds are my addition and give this cake a lovely nutty texture.

Serves 8

200g butter, softened, plus a little extra for greasing
400g eating or garden apples
grated zest and juice of 1 lemon
300g soft light brown sugar
3 eggs
3 tbsp sour cream
1 tsp almond extract
200g gluten-free self-raising flour
1 tsp gluten-free baking powder
100g ground almonds
50g flaked almonds
icing sugar, for dusting

Preheat your oven to 180°C/160°C Fan/Gas Mark 4/350°F. Grease and line a 30 x 23cm/12 x 9in rectangular baking tin with butter and baking paper.

Peel, core and cube the apples, then place them in a large bowl with the lemon juice and 1 tablespoon of the brown sugar and mix.

In a stand mixer, beat together the butter and remaining brown sugar until light and fluffy. Add the eggs, one by one, along with the sour cream, lemon zest and almond extract. Sift in the flour and baking powder, then fold through until all the flour is incorporated. Add the ground almonds and fold in. Finally, drain the apples, tip them into the cake batter and fold in. Pour the batter into the prepared cake tin and tap the tin gently on the work surface to settle any bubbles.

Bake in the centre of the oven for 1 hour. After an hour, sprinkle over the flaked almonds and bake for a further 10 minutes. The cake should look well-risen and golden, like a rustic, Dorset-style apple cake.

Remove from the oven and leave the cake to cool in tin. Before serving, remove from tin and dust with icing sugar.

VEGAN CHOCOLATE HAZELNUT CAKE

GF

There is a huge vegan movement in Poland, and I have had the benefit of sampling plenty of vegan cakes and plant-based alternatives both in Krakow and on the Warsaw food scene. Warsaw has even been named the third most vegan-friendly city in the world, according to the website Notes from Poland, so there is much to explore, especially on the cake front. In Krakow, I visited a quaint café on Józefa Sarego, which was close to my rental apartment and there I had the most delicious vegan chocolate cake. This is my variation and I like to use my friend Urszula's fruit vinegar, Octovnia, made in Poland. This is a really easy cake to throw together and is mostly made with store-cupboard ingredients.

Serves 8–10

100g gluten-free self-raising flour

100g ground hazelnuts (or use ground almonds)

50g ground oat flour (or gluten-free rolled oats, blitzed)

1 tsp bicarbonate of soda

125g soft light brown sugar

1 ripe banana, mashed

a pinch of salt

1 tsp vanilla bean extract

3 tsp good-quality vegan fruit vinegar

60ml vegetable oil

300ml oat milk

100g good-quality vegan dark chocolate, melted

For the topping:

100g good-quality vegan dark chocolate, chopped

1 tsp grated orange zest, plus extra to decorate

100ml vegan/plant-based double cream

a few whole and chopped hazelnuts

Preheat your oven to 170°C/150°C Fan/Gas Mark 3½/340°F. Line a 23 x 23cm/9 x 9in square baking tin with baking paper.

Place all the ingredients (apart from the chocolate) in a bowl and stir together with a whisk. Once combined, pour in the melted chocolate and stir again. Pour the mixture into your prepared tin and bake in the oven for 45–50 minutes until it is firm to touch. Leave the cake to cool completely.

For the topping, melt the chocolate, add the orange zest and pour in the vegan cream. Whisk until smooth and pour over the cake, then top with a few whole and chopped hazelnuts and a little more grated orange zest.

The cake will keep well in a tin for a couple of days, although it is best eaten fresh, with an extra splash of vegan cream.

TORT AMBASADOR

I am very lucky to have been invited to the Embassy of the Republic of Poland in London a number of times, to mark special occasions and Polish national holidays, such as the Constitution of 3rd May (adopted in 1791 by the Polish-Lithuanian Commonwealth) or Polish Independence Day celebrated on 11th November. It makes all the Saturdays I spent at Polish school learning Polish, during my childhood, worthwhile, and it always gives me a wonderful opportunity to soak up the atmosphere inside a building that holds so much historical significance for Poles in London. While I have yet to turn up with a cake, if I had to choose one, I'd pick the *tort ambasador* for obvious reasons. The French version of this is *gâteau l'ambassadeur*, so I am guessing that it's not just the Poles who like to honour their ambassadors with a cake. Diplomacy is an art form, and in all cases, I find everything is made better with cake. Call it cultural diplomacy, if you will. There are a few variations on this recipe; some include a jelly layer or raisins, but I like to include cherries, and if they happen to be soaked in a little alcohol, so much the better.

Serves 8–10

For the chocolate sponge:

120ml vegetable oil or mild, light olive oil, plus extra for greasing

200g soft light brown sugar

2 eggs

1 tsp vanilla bean extract

240g sour cream

200g self-raising flour

75g cocoa powder

1 tsp baking powder

1 tsp bicarbonate of soda

240ml freshly brewed hot black tea

For the cherry chocolate filling:

500ml double cream

2 tbsp icing sugar

2 tbsp cocoa powder

100g canned cherries in syrup or alcohol, drained (reserve the syrup/alcohol for the soak)

For the peaches and cream:

500ml double cream

2 tbsp icing sugar

1 x 420g can peach slices in syrup, drained and chopped

Preheat your oven to 180°C/160°C Fan/Gas Mark 4/350°F. Grease and line two 20cm/8in round cake tins with oil and baking paper.

In a stand mixer, beat the oil and brown sugar until it starts to thicken. Add the eggs, one by one, and the vanilla. Stir in the sour cream. Sift in the flour, cocoa powder, baking powder and bicarbonate of soda, and stir through until there are no lumps. Finally, pour in the hot tea and mix again thoroughly.

Pour the batter into the prepared tins, smooth it out and tap them gently on the work top to settle any bubbles. Bake for 30–35 minutes until an inserted skewer comes out clean. Cool completely in the tins.

For the cherry chocolate filling, whip the cream, adding the icing sugar and cocoa powder until it thickens. Stir through the drained cherries.

For the peaches and cream, whip the cream, adding the icing sugar until thick, then stir through half of the chopped peaches.

To assemble the cake, line one of your tins with clingfilm and place one of the sponge layers in the bottom. Brush over some of the reserved cherry syrup/alcohol, or use some peach syrup. Spread over the cherry chocolate filling, then place the second layer of sponge on top. Brush with a little more syrup/alcohol, then spread the peaches and cream mixture over the top, smoothing it out with a palette knife. Place the whole cake in the refrigerator to chill.

When you are ready to serve, carefully remove the cake from the tin and place it on a cake stand. Decorate with the remaining chopped peaches and some grated milk chocolate.

CARNIVAL TREATS

DOUGHNUTS WITH CUSTARD OR ADVOCAAT CREAM

If you've got yourself an egg-rich, brioche-like, buttery, sugary doughnut, why not fill it with more eggs, cream and booze? Class it as a pre-Lenten blow out. For the doughnuts, use the recipe on page 90. Custard-filled doughnuts are also particularly good with a chocolate glaze, so if you want to use that, you can find the recipe on page 44. As to the advocaat cream, there is a Polish version involving vodka, which is surprisingly popular around the doughnut shops of Warsaw. Advocaat is, of course, a bright-yellow Dutch liqueur made with eggs, brandy and cream. It is a bit like drinking a boozy custard, and it's particularly good served warm with cream on top (also known as a *bombardino* in Italy – an eggnog-style cocktail with an additional slug of brandy that you often have when skiing). *Advocaat* is the Dutch word for lawyer, although the origins of the drink are thought to have originated in Brazil, where it was made from avocado and called *abacate*. Since avocados were not available in Europe, they made it using eggs. The Poles have their own version, called *ajerkoniak*, or *adwokat* (also the word for lawyer), but they make theirs with vodka, or *spiritus* – a 100%-proof clear spirit, which I would only recommend using with caution. Anyway, to make the most delicious doughnut filling, you make a *krem adwokatowy*, or advocaat cream, giving you a boozy custard-filled doughnut. If you want to go all-out, you can make your own home-made liqueur. If you simply want to buy a bottle and skip out the custard stage, there's an even speedier version below using mascarpone cheese.

Makes 8 filled doughnuts

1 x quantity of Classic Polish Doughnuts (page 90, omitting the fillings and toppings)

1 x quantity of Pastry Cream (page 26)

3 tbsp advocaat liqueur (optional) (store-bought or see page 178 for a home-made version)

icing sugar, for dusting

For a quick krem adwokatowy (advocaat cream):

200ml double cream

250g mascarpone cheese

150ml advocaat liqueur (store-bought or see page 178 for a home-made version)

4 tbsp icing sugar

2 tsp cornflour

Make the doughnuts according to the instructions on page 92, but do not fill them or top them.

Make the pastry cream according to the instructions on page 26. It can be used to fill your doughnuts as is, but for an advocaat version, when all the butter has been whisked in, stir in the advocaat liqueur and keep it chilled until you need to fill your doughnuts.

For a quick version of advocaat cream, put the double cream into a bowl with the mascarpone and advocaat. Sift in the icing sugar and cornflour, then beat together until thickened, and use to fill your doughnuts (see page 90 for filling method).

Dust with icing sugar to serve.

MINI VEGAN POPPY SEED DOUGHNUTS

For this recipe, you'll need a little mini doughnut tin, which has twelve holes, or you can use a medium tin with six holes, in which case, bake them for a couple of minutes longer. These are a little sweet hit and very easy to make in just one bowl. If you don't have a doughnut tin, you can use a mini cupcake tin.

Makes 12 mini or 6 regular doughnuts, depending on the size of the tin

spray oil, for the tin
250g self-raising flour
100g caster sugar
125ml oat milk
30g vegan butter
1 tsp vanilla bean paste
2 tbsp poppy seeds
icing sugar or 50g good-quality vegan dark chocolate, melted, to decorate

Preheat your oven to 180°C/160°C Fan/Gas Mark 4/350°F. Spray a 12-hole mini doughnut tin (or a 6-hole medium doughnut tin) with oil.

Mix the flour, sugar, oat milk, vegan butter, vanilla and poppy seeds together in a bowl using a balloon whisk until combined. It's easier if you spoon the batter into a piping bag fitted with a round nozzle; otherwise, use a teaspoon.

Pipe (or spoon) the batter into the doughnut tin, filling the holes half to three-quarters full. Bake in the oven for 10 minutes (or 12 minutes if using a medium tin). They will be firm to the touch.

Leave to cool slightly in the tin and then turn out onto a wire rack. You can dust these with icing sugar or dip them into a little melted dark chocolate to serve, whilst warm.

QUICK CREAM CHEESE DOUGHNUT BITES

These little mini doughnuts, or *pączki serowe,* are perfect for times when a very quick and tasty dessert is needed and you want the hit of a classic Polish doughnut but don't have the time to prove and wait for them. They are made with cream cheese, or curd cheese, which is Polish *twaróg.* Sometimes, I make the Croatian version of these, which are called *fritule* and have raisins in them, a little brandy or rum, along with citrus zest. In Croatia, you might have these at Christmas. In Italy, during carnival, you would have *zeppole* or *fritole.* In Germany, they are made with quark cheese.

Makes around 20

250g cream cheese or twaróg or
 twaróg sernikowy *(see page 20)*

100g thick, natural yogurt

3 egg yolks

1 tsp vanilla bean paste

60g caster sugar

250g plain flour

2 tsp bicarbonate of soda

1 tsp baking powder

1 tbsp white wine vinegar (fruit
 vinegar works well, too)

500ml rapeseed oil, for deep-frying

icing sugar, for dusting

If you are using Polish cream cheese, mash it with a fork or a potato masher, or whizz it in a food processor, to make sure it is smooth. If you have *twaróg sernikowy,* cream cheese or curd cheese, it will already be smooth.

Mix together the cheese, yogurt, egg yolks and vanilla until you have a smooth mixture. Add the caster sugar and stir, then fold in the flour, bicarbonate of soda, baking powder and vinegar. You should have a batter with a dropping consistency.

Heat the oil in a large, heavy-based pan to 175°C/345°F (use a sugar thermometer), or until a cube of bread browns within 20 seconds. Quickly drop teaspoonfuls of the batter into the oil until you have around 8–10 cooking. Deep-fry the mini doughnuts on all sides, until they are golden brown, 1–2 minutes in total. Carefully take the doughnuts out with a slotted spoon and drain in a bowl lined with kitchen paper. Repeat to deep-fry the rest of the doughnut bites.

Dust with icing sugar to serve.

PĄCZKI

Classic Polish Doughnuts with Jam and Icing

In Poland, during the pre-Lent or carnival season, we celebrate *Tłusty Czwartek*, which means Fat Thursday, also known as Doughnut Day. It is the equivalent to Mardi Gras or Shrove Tuesday. There is always a fierce competition in Warsaw to be named the best doughnut shop. Polish doughnuts have a high egg yolk content with added butter, so they are richer than traditional doughnuts. I have noticed something of a trend for brioche doughnuts recently, and Polish doughnuts are pretty close, the common element being eggs and butter. Polish doughnuts are traditionally filled with rose jam, plum jam or custard, but if you take a trip to Poland, you'll find all sorts of fillings and flavours, including citrus, rose, cinnamon and advocaat. They can be sugared, usually with icing sugar, or lightly iced. I'm always reminded of a snowy trip to the mountain resort town of Zakopane, where there is a *pączkarnia* (doughnut shop) on Krupówki, with a window filled with doughnuts and a lady by the window frying them. It's absolutely mesmerising. On a cold, snowy day, there's nothing better than sinking your teeth into a freshly fried and filled doughnut, although it's hard to eat just one. Incidentally, eating one doughnut, or a single *pączek,* is considered to be bad luck, so make sure you eat at least two! Making doughnuts at home isn't very difficult, you might just need a little practise and take care when frying.

Makes 8 large doughnuts

250g plain flour, plus extra for dusting

30g fresh yeast, crumbled (or 14g active dry yeast)

50g caster sugar

250ml lukewarm milk

250g strong white bread flour

1 tbsp sunflower oil, plus extra for greasing

a pinch of salt

4 egg yolks

2 tsp vodka

70g butter, melted

To finish:

about 1 litre vegetable oil, for deep-frying

jam of your choice, for filling

250g icing sugar

50ml water or rosewater

edible dried rose petals or citrus peel, to decorate (optional)

continued over-leaf

For the starter, place 3 tablespoons of the plain flour in a bowl, crumble in the fresh yeast (or sprinkle in the dried yeast), add 1 tablespoon of the sugar and stir in half of the lukewarm milk. Cover with a clean cloth and leave in a warm place for 10–15 minutes.

When the starter has risen, sift the remaining flours into a large bowl, add the starter, the remaining sugar, the oil and a pinch of salt, and bring together by hand or with a silicone spoon. Add the rest of the milk, the egg yolks, vodka and melted butter, then knead the dough, or use a stand mixer fitted with a dough hook, until it becomes smooth and elastic. This will take around 5 minutes. Carefully scrape any dough off the hook or from around the bowl. Tip the dough out, rub a little oil around the bowl, then put the dough back in and cover with clingfilm. Leave in a warm place (this could even be a low oven at 35°C/95°F) for 1 hour.

Once your dough has risen, sprinkle some flour onto a large board and tip the dough out onto it. Roll out to 2.5cm/1in thick, then use a 7cm/2¾in cutter or a glass to cut out round pieces of dough. Shape into small slightly flattened balls, lightly rounding the edges. Space the dough pieces out on a tray, cover with a clean cloth and leave them in a warm place, for a further half an hour.

Heat the oil for deep-frying in a large, heavy-based pan to 175°C/345°F (use a sugar thermometer), or until a cube of bread browns within 20 seconds. Line a plate with kitchen paper and set nearby. Deep-fry 3–4 doughnuts at a time for 2–3 minutes on each side, gently flipping once. You should end up with a golden doughnut with a lighter ring around the middle. Remove with a slotted spoon to the lined plate. It is best to try deep-frying one doughnut first, then leave it to cool slightly before pulling it apart. You want to check that the dough is cooked all the way through. Call it a cook's treat.

Once you have fried all the doughnuts, leave them to cool slightly before filling them with jam. To do this, I make a hole in the side with a chopstick, then use a piping bag fitted with a plain nozzle to pipe the jam into the middle.

For the icing, mix the icing sugar with the water or rosewater until you have a thick, but pourable liquid. Pour a little over each doughnut and serve. They look pretty if you sprinkle them with dried rose petals or a little citrus peel.

KARPATKA

Carpathian Mountain Cake

I mention in Chapter 2, that the Napoleon Cake, or *Napoleonka,* was said to have been a favourite of Pope John II, and that it is also sometimes known as a *kremowka* or a *papieska kremowka* – papal cream cake. The *karpatka* is a little step up from that one, and is also known as a Carpathian mountain cake, named after the Karpaty mountain range. The dough (in this case a choux pastry) creates the effect of mountains, and the icing sugar on top represents the snow. There are variations dating back to the 1950s and '60s, which is the sort of time my parents began making their first return to Poland, after the Second World War (their first trip back was in 1952, and I have a memorable photograph of my mum, dad and two cousins standing outside the Teatr Narodowy, or National Theatre, in Warsaw). I like to think that, just after that photo, they went off to sit in a café in Warsaw to eat a slice of *karpatka*. The filling is a *krem budyniowy* (pastry cream), which you'll find in Baking Basics on page 26. For the choux, I use equal parts of water and milk. I sometimes like to add a layer of rose petal jam, but you can use any marmalade or preserve you fancy. The author of *Polska*, Zuza Zak, adds vanilla and cardamom to hers, which is also a lovely touch. If you can master the choux, you can go on to make éclairs!

Serves 12

2 x quantity of Pastry Cream/
  Krem Budyniowy (page 26)
100g marmalade or any fruit
  preserve of your choice
icing sugar, for dusting
toasted flaked almonds (optional)

For the choux pastry:

125ml water
125ml milk
1 tsp caster sugar
1 tsp vanilla bean paste
a pinch of salt
110g butter
200g plain flour
1 tsp baking powder
4 eggs

continued over-leaf

Preheat your oven to 180°C/160°C Fan/Gas Mark 4/350°F. Line two 30 x 23cm/12 x 9in baking trays with baking paper.

For the choux pastry, combine the water, milk, sugar, vanilla, salt and butter in a small pan and bring to a gentle boil, taking care that the milk doesn't scald. Once the mixture comes to the boil, add the flour in one go along with the baking powder and be ready to mix this vigorously (I use a wooden spoon). You will end up with a ball of dough that is a little sticky, but keep beating. Beat until it comes away from the sides of the pan, then leave to cool completely.

Transfer the ball of dough to a large, clean bowl, or use a stand mixer or food processor. Add the whole eggs to the dough, one by one. Make sure each egg is well mixed into the dough before adding the next one. You should end up with a smooth, thick mixture, somewhere between a batter and a dough.

Divide the mixture across the two baking trays. Don't smooth it out – you are looking for an uneven layer to create the mountains. As it bakes, ridges and furrows will form. Bake for 30–35 minutes until it is golden and well-risen. Switch off the oven and open the door, allowing the steam to escape and the pastry to sit for a few minutes. After this time, take the pastry out of the oven and leave to cool completely.

You can now make the pastry cream filling, following the method on page 26. Leave the filling to cool, too, covering the surface with clingfilm so that a skin does not form.

Place one of the choux pastry layers onto a serving platter and spread over a thin layer of marmalade or fruit preserve. Spread over the pastry cream, then place the second layer of choux pastry on the top. Add a sprinkle of toasted almonds and dust with icing sugar, if you like. Cut into rectangles to serve.

FAWORKI/CHRUSTY

Angel Wings

The best thing about visiting a Polish aunt or grandmother, especially during the carnival or festive season, is seeing plates piled high with angel wings, which can be called *chrusty, chruściki* or *faworki* in Poland. They are named that way because they resemble ribbons or twigs. *Faworki* refers to the colourful ribbons you spot on traditional blouses, while *chruściki* refers to the dried branches of trees. In Italy, during carnival time, you get *chiacchiere*, and in Portugal I have seen similar treats covered in honey and walnuts. They are known as *favorki* in Belarus, or *khvorost*, in Russia, meaning 'twigs'. The Polish version is thin pastry twists that are dusted liberally with icing sugar. Like doughnuts, they can take a little practise, but you generally can't go wrong once these are fried. If they are crumbly, this means they are good.

Makes 25–30

240g plain flour, plus extra for dusting

2 tbsp icing sugar, plus extra for dusting

½ tsp baking powder

a pinch of salt

4 egg yolks

50ml sour cream

3 tbsp vodka

grated zest of 1 lemon

1 tbsp butter, melted

1 tsp vanilla bean paste

about 1 litre vegetable oil, for deep-frying

Use a stand mixer fitted with a paddle attachment if you have one; otherwise, a large bowl. Add the flour, icing sugar, baking powder and salt to the bowl, then add the egg yolks, sour cream, vodka, lemon zest, melted butter and vanilla. Mix together until a loose dough forms. Tip the dough onto a floured surface, form into a ball, then wrap it in clingfilm and chill in the refrigerator for up to 1 hour.

Sprinkle some extra flour onto a board, cut the dough in half and wrap the second piece in clingfilm while you work. Knead the dough for 5 minutes. If the dough is a little sticky, sprinkle over some extra flour. You do not need to be gentle with this dough and, in fact, some Polish cooks beat it with a rolling pin to work it. Do this with both pieces, then wrap again in clingfilm and leave to settle for 10 minutes.

After this time, sprinkle some more flour over the board. Working with one half at a time, roll out the dough as thinly as you can on the board. Ideally, it should be paper thin. Lift the dough occasionally to make sure it is not sticking to the board. Take a sharp knife or a pastry cutter and cut the dough into 3cm/1 ¼in-thick long strips, then cut each strip in half so you have two shorter pieces. Make a 3cm/1¼in slit down the centre of each strip of dough. This is the fun part: working with one piece at a time, pull one end of the dough through the slit you have made and keep pulling until you have a twist. Repeat with all of the dough strips, including the second ball of dough.

Heat the oil in a large, heavy-based pan to 175°C/345°F (use a sugar thermometer), or until a cube of bread browns within 20 seconds. Line a plate with kitchen paper and set nearby. Deep-fry 3–4 pastry ribbons at a time for 15 seconds. Don't overcrowd the pan. Using a fork or spoon, carefully flip the pastry twists until they are light, golden brown. They will puff up slightly. Drain the pastry twists on the kitchen paper, then arrange on a large plate and dust very liberally with icing sugar.

Carnival Treats

EKLERY

Éclairs with Banana and Caramel

The éclair was the invention of French patisserie chef, Marie-Antoine Carême, but of course the Poles have their own version, called *eklery* or *eklerki*. You can find them in high-end patisseries in Poland, including at my favourite café within the Hotel Bristol in Warsaw, or at Lukullus or A.Blikle, where you'll find many other delightful treats. If you're not sitting in a café in Warsaw watching the world go by, you're missing a trick.

Makes 12

1 x quantity of Choux Pastry, using only 2 eggs (see Karpatka recipe, page 93)

For the filling:

600ml double cream (or use Pastry Cream/krem budyniowy from Baking Basics, page 26)

1 tbsp icing sugar

2 tbsp kajmak or masa krówkowa or thick caramel

3–4 ripe bananas

200g good-quality dark chocolate, chopped

Preheat your oven to 180°C/160°C Fan/Gas Mark 4/350°F. Line a baking sheet with baking paper.

Follow the steps for making the choux pastry on page 95, but using 2 eggs instead of 4 eggs. Fit a piping bag with a plain nozzle and transfer the choux pastry mixture into the piping bag. Pipe 12 lines of choux onto the lined baking sheet, each about 12cm/4½in long, leaving a good gap in between each line. Bake in the oven for 15–20 minutes until golden, then open the oven door and leave the éclairs inside for a further few minutes. Take out of the oven and leave to cool completely on a wire rack.

Once cooled, halve the éclairs lengthways. Whip the double cream with the icing sugar, thens stir in the caramel until combined. For the best effect, fill a piping bag (fitted with a plain or open star nozzle) with the mixture and pipe the cream carefully onto the bottom half of each éclair (alternatively, you can fill them with pastry cream). Thinly slice the bananas and top the filling with a few slices, then top with the other pastry halves.

To finish, melt the chocolate gently, leave to cool for ten minutes, then spread or drizzle a little melted chocolate onto each éclair.

JAM-FILLED COOKIES

Little jam-filled cookies to melt the heart, these are an easy carnival treat to make, especially with the children to help.

Makes around 30

200g plain flour or spelt flour
100g cornflour or potato flour
100g ground almonds
100g caster sugar
a pinch of salt
1 tsp vanilla bean paste
grated zest of ½ lemon
180g soft butter or margarine
100g jam or fruit preserve of
   your choice

Line a large baking tray with baking paper.

Bring all the ingredients (apart from the jam) together in a bowl or a food processor. A soft ball of dough should form. Cut the dough in half and roll into two long logs. Place them on the lined baking tray and chill in the refrigerator for 1 hour.

Preheat your oven to 180°C/160°C Fan/Gas Mark 4/350°F.

Take the cookie dough from the refrigerator and cut each log into 1cm/½in wide slices. You should get around 30 little discs. Place the discs back onto the lined tray (you may need to do this in batches unless you have more trays). Using a teaspoon, make a little indent in the centre of each disc and fill each one with a small amount of jam.

Bake the cookies in the oven for 12–15 minutes (in two batches if necessary). Leave to cool slightly on baking tray before eating.

APPLE RINGS IN YEASTED BATTER

When my grandmother, Babcia Tekla, settled in the UK after the war (having escaped from Wołyń in Poland, making her way with a young family through Austria and Italy), she lived in a Polish resettlement camp in the north of England, near Nantwich. This is where lots of Polish children, including my Mama and her siblings, attended makeshift Polish schools, before eventually settling into the wider British community in the mid-1950s. They lived on rations and they sometimes had a little space to grow vegetables and keep a couple of chickens. They would also pick berries and forage for other fruit, such as apples. When I was little, Babcia Tekla would tell me that she would save up some of her ration stamps, so that she could exchange them for luxury items, such as flour, sugar and yeast. Then, she would make treats, such as these, on the stove.

Serves 4

4–6 eating apples

a little lemon juice

160g self-raising flour

17g fresh yeast, crumbled (or 7g fast-action dried yeast)

125g caster sugar

120ml lukewarm milk

1 egg yolk

vegetable oil, for frying

icing sugar, for dusting

Peel the apples, core them and slice into 1cm/½in-thick rings. Toss them in a bowl with a little lemon juice so that they don't turn brown.

Put 2 tablespoons of the flour into a mixing bowl, crumble or sprinkle in the yeast, add 1 tablespoon of the sugar and a little of the lukewarm milk and whisk together. Leave this mixture somewhere warm for 10 minutes until bubbles form.

Mix the egg yolk with the rest of the milk, then add the rest of the flour and sugar to the yeast mixture and whisk in the yolk and milk until you have a smooth batter.

Heat a 3cm/1¼ in depth of oil in a large, wide frying pan until hot.

Drain the apples. Dip each apple ring into the batter, then fry them (around 4 rings at a time) in the hot oil until they are golden. The oil should be just bubbling – keep an eye on the heat so that the apples in batter don't get too brown too quickly. Drain on a plate lined with kitchen paper and repeat until all the apple rings have been fried.

Dust with icing sugar and serve immediately.

FLORENTINE CAKE

There is a recipe for *ciasto Florentynki* in a Polish recipe book from 1874, written by the author Florentyna Niewiarowska, and it begins with 'half a pound of sugar with the scent of orange or lemon'. This is such a lovely opening to a recipe; in fact, it always reminds me to keep a jar of sugar scented with orange peel, and one of sugar scented with lemon peel, in my pantry. The original recipe calls for clarified butter, while I use melted butter, and it doesn't call for chocolate, but I find a drizzle doesn't go amiss.

Serves 8

225g Lemon Sugar (see Baking Basics, page 21)

8 eggs, separated

225g self-raising flour

225g butter, melted

2 tbsp caster sugar

200g flaked almonds

2 tbsp water

75g good-quality dark chocolate, melted

Preheat your oven to 180°C/160°C Fan/Gas Mark 4/350°F. Line a 30 x 23cm/12 x 9in rectangular baking tin with baking paper.

Beat the lemon sugar with the egg yolks in a bowl until pale and fluffy, then stir in the flour and melted butter until combined.

In a spotlessly clean bowl, whisk the egg whites until stiff peaks form, then add half of the egg whites to the batter.

Pour the batter into the lined tin and spread evenly. Spread the remaining half of the egg whites over the top until you have a smooth layer. Add the sugar to the almonds, then add the water and stir. Spread the almonds evenly over the top of the egg whites.

Bake in the oven for 25 minutes until the almonds are golden brown and glistening, then remove from the oven and leave to cool completely in the tin.

To finish, remove from the tin, cut the cake into rectangles and drizzle over a little melted chocolate.

APPLE AND ALMOND BUNS

There is a beautiful café in Krakow that I frequented recently with my friend Monika, called Fornir Kawiarnia on Ulica Długa. It's the kind of café I would be in almost every day, if I lived in Krakow. They serve delicious open sandwiches with a variety of toppings – we had roasted pumpkin with almonds, and pâté with home-pickled gherkins and pink peppercorns, followed by yeasted buns filled with apples and caramel, washed down with seasonal pumpkin lattés. Monika and I sat and ate in silence. When we tore open the deep-filled buns, we gasped – the autumn leaves fell around us and, as per the little warning note attached to the nearby tree, a walnut fell on my head. We laughed as deeply as our buns had been filled with apples. These are my take, although they won't be half as good. You could drizzle these with caramel sauce, for an extra treat.

Makes 12

25g fresh yeast, crumbled (or 14g instant dried yeast)

300g plain flour, plus a little extra for dusting

2 tbsp icing sugar

200ml lukewarm milk, plus a little extra to glaze

75g butter, melted

1 egg

1 x quantity of Stewed Apples (from Baking Basics, page 25), cooled

a few flaked almonds to decorate the top of each bun

Put the yeast in a mixing bowl with 1 tablespoon of the flour, 1 tablespoon of the icing sugar and a little of the lukewarm milk and whisk together. Leave in a warm place for 10 minutes.

Sift the rest of the flour into the yeast mixture, add the melted butter, the remaining tablespoon of icing sugar, the rest of the milk and the egg, and mix together. Turn out and knead on a board sprinkled with a little flour until you have a soft and elastic dough (or use a stand mixer fitted with a dough hook). Put the dough back into the bowl, cover with a clean cloth and leave in a warm place to rise for 30 minutes.

Turn the dough back out onto a board sprinkled with flour, knead and roll out a little. Cut the dough into 12 roughly equal portions. Place a good tablespoon of stewed apples onto each piece of dough, then fold each in half and form the dough around the apple filling to enclose it. Line a baking tray with baking paper. Place the filled buns on the tray and cover again with a cloth and leave in a warm place for a further 30 minutes.

Preheat your oven to 200°C/180°C Fan/Gas Mark 6/400°F.

Before baking, glaze the buns with a little milk before sprinkling with a few flaked almonds.

Bake the buns in the oven for 20 minutes until they are risen and golden. Leave to cool slightly on baking tray before eating.

SEASONAL

Easter, Christmas and Other Occasions

MARBLED CHOCOLATE AND VANILLA BUNDT

In Poland, a traditional *babka* is a yeasted recipe, but this one is a very simple no-yeast bake, enriched with eggs. The yeasted (and sometimes plaited) *babka* originated in the Jewish communities of Eastern Europe in the early 19th century. They were a cross between a bread and a cake. Unlike the twisted-loaf shape of a Jewish *babka*, the Polish 'cake' version is baked in a bundt tin. This one has a luxurious, glossy, chocolate glaze. For a Jewish-style, plaited *babka*, try the Wild Blueberry and Babka Loaf on page 156.

Serves 8

125g butter, at room temperature, plus 1 tbsp melted for greasing

100g cornflour, plus 1 tbsp extra for dusting

150g caster sugar

60ml vegetable oil

4 eggs

1 tsp vanilla bean paste

3 tbsp natural yogurt

125g self-raising flour

1 tsp baking powder

2 tbsp cocoa powder

For the chocolate glaze:

2 tbsp butter

100g good-quality dark chocolate, chopped

100g icing sugar

1 tbsp runny honey

2 tbsp boiling water

Preheat your oven to 180°C/160°C Fan/Gas Mark 4/350°F. Brush the inside of a 2.4 litre/10 cup bundt tin with the melted butter, then dust with the tablespoon of cornflour.

In a bowl or a stand mixer, beat the butter, sugar and oil together for 3–4 minutes until soft and fluffy. Add the eggs, one by one, and beat slowly. Add the vanilla bean paste and yogurt. Using a metal spoon, fold in the self-raising flour, cornflour and baking powder. Divide the mixture in half, add the cocoa powder to one half and mix until combined.

Using a large spoon, spoon some of the vanilla batter into the bottom of the prepared bundt tin, then add dollops of the chocolate batter. Finish with the vanilla batter.

Bake in the oven for 40 minutes, then remove from the oven and leave to cool in the tin before carefully turning it out onto a serving plate.

To make the glaze, melt the butter and chocolate in a pan, then stir through the icing sugar, honey and boiling water, and mix until smooth. The glaze will stay glossy if you eat it immediately, but will turn matt if left, therefore make and pour over the glaze when you are ready to serve the bundt.

ALMOND BUNDT WITH ROASTED RHUBARB GLAZE

This is a crumbly, buttery bundt cake with a hint of almond. I usually make a roasted rhubarb glaze, as rhubarb comes into season in April, but if you are making this later in the year, you can roast some plums and make a glaze in the same way. Decorate with dried cornflowers, primroses or lavender. You can use the leftover syrup to make a rhubarb or plum martini. Any leftover fruit can be eaten as a compote or over yogurt for breakfast.

Serves 8

a little vegetable oil, for greasing

1 tbsp fresh, white breadcrumbs or plain flour, for the tin

175g butter, at room temperature

140g caster sugar

3 tbsp water

3 eggs

grated zest of 1 lemon

2 tsp runny honey

1 tsp almond extract

100g self-raising flour

40g potato flour or cornflour

100g ground almonds

edible fresh flowers, to decorate

For the rhubarb glaze:

500g fresh rhubarb (or plums, stoned)

100g caster sugar

50g icing sugar

Preheat your oven to 200°C/180°C Fan/Gas Mark 6/400°F. Line a large roasting pan with baking paper.

First, make the rhubarb glaze. Wash the rhubarb, cut it into small pieces on the diagonal and tumble into the lined roasting pan. Sprinkle over the caster sugar and 2 tablespoons of water, cover with foil and bake in the oven for 15 minutes. The rhubarb should have released lots of juices and there should be some syrup in the bottom of the pan. If it needs a little longer, drizzle over another tablespoon of water and roast for a further 10 minutes. Set aside to cool.

Brush the inside of a 2.4 litre/10 cup bundt tin with a little oil, then dust with the breadcrumbs or plain flour. Turn the oven down to 160°C/140°C Fan/Gas Mark 3/325°F.

Beat the butter and caster sugar together until fluffy. Add the eggs, one by one, then add the lemon zest, honey and almond extract and mix again. Finally, add the self-raising flour, potato flour or cornflour and ground almonds and mix gently until just combined.

Spoon the batter into the prepared tin and bake for 40–45 minutes, until an inserted skewer comes out completely clean. It should be firm to the touch and the *babka* will be a golden brown colour all over. Leave to cool in the tin, before carefully turning it out onto a serving plate.

To make the glaze, drain the syrup from the roasted rhubarb pieces. Mix the syrup with the icing sugar and pour it over the bundt. Decorate with a few pieces of the roasted rhubarb and some edible flowers.

EASY BUTTERMILK BUNDT WITH FRUIT

GF

This is an easy bundt cake, which I most often make with gluten-free self-raising flour and ground almonds. It has a lovely crumb and is very adaptable, suiting the addition of most fruits (berries, chopped apricots, chopped apples, etc.). To make buttermilk, you can stir 2 teaspoons of lemon juice into 240ml of milk and set it aside for a few minutes before using.

Serves 8

a little melted butter or vegetable oil, for greasing

200g gluten-free self-raising flour, plus extra for dusting

225g soft light brown sugar or caster sugar

4 eggs

125ml light vegetable oil

1 tsp vanilla bean paste or almond extract

grated zest of ½ lemon or orange

225g buttermilk (or use sour cream)

140g ground almonds

½ tsp bicarbonate of soda

a pinch of salt

300g berries, such as blueberries, or chopped apples (peeled and cored) or pears (optional)

icing sugar, for dusting

Preheat your oven to 160°C/140°C Fan/Gas Mark 3/325°F. Brush the inside of a 2 litre/8 cup bundt tin with a little melted butter or oil and dust with a little flour.

In the bowl of a stand mixer fitted with a paddle attachment, beat the sugar and eggs together until fluffy. Slowly add the oil, then the vanilla bean paste or almond extract and the lemon or orange zest. Stir in the buttermilk.

Sift the flour into a separate bowl, add the ground almonds, bicarbonate of soda and salt and stir well to combine. Add this to the cake batter and fold in slowly until all the flour is incorporated. If you are using berries or fruit, tip them in now and stir gently to combine.

Carefully spoon the batter into your prepared tin and bake in the oven for 40 minutes, or until a skewer inserted into the middle of the cake comes out completely clean. Leave the cake to cool in the tin, before carefully turning it out onto a serving plate.

Dust with icing sugar and serve.

BABKA

Easter Yeasted Bundt

During spring and Eastertime in Poland, *babas* or *babkas* begin to take centre stage. They are usually of the yeasted variety, often studded with candied fruit and glazed with icing. Easter is one of the most important Christian holidays in Poland and it is a beautiful time to visit, as you'll see lots of processions in the streets, with tall and colourful palms and plenty of interesting food at the table. Once Easter arrives, the Lent period, where fasting takes place, is over and butter and sugar are back. If you are preparing a basket for Easter Saturday, you'll usually find a *baba*, or a *babka*, nestled inside. While layer cakes came to Poland later, likely thanks to the Italian Queen Bona who married a Polish King, *babas* and *mazurek* cakes are highly traditional and feature in the oldest Polish recipe books. *Babas* would be baked by the lady of the house and by all the women around her. If your *baba* were to sink, you would certainly lose face. A description of an Easter feast during the reign of Ladislaus (Władysław) IV, King of Poland and Grand Duke of Lithuania, described 52 whole cakes, one for each week of the year, while 'behind this there were 365 *babas*, that is as many as there are days in a year'. We'd better get baking. The name *babka* derives from *baba*, which is short for *babcia*, meaning grandmother. Some say the fluted bundt shape of a Polish *babka* also resembles a grandmother's skirt.

Serves 8

500g strong white bread flour

14g fresh yeast, crumbled (or 7g instant dried yeast)

200g caster sugar

6 eggs

a pinch of salt

400g butter, at room temperature, cubed

grated zest of 1 lemon or orange

1 tsp vanilla bean paste

100g mixed peel

100g raisins (soaked in a little rum, vodka or water and drained)

a little vegetable oil, for greasing

1 tbsp breadcrumbs or plain flour, for the tin

2 tbsp water

50g icing sugar

a few drops of natural food colouring (optional)

Sift the flour into the bowl of a stand mixer, ideally fitted with a dough hook. Add the yeast and the sugar, and begin to mix. Add the eggs, very slowly, one by one, until incorporated. The dough should start to come away from the bowl, but it will still be quite sticky. Add a pinch of salt and the butter, and keep kneading/mixing for 5 minutes. Add the citrus zest, vanilla, mixed peel and raisins and knead again just until incorporated. The mixture will remain quite wet. Cover the bowl with a clean cloth and leave it somewhere warm to prove for 1 hour. It should double in size.

After an hour, mix gently with a wooden spoon to knock some of the air out. Brush the inside of a 2.4 litre/10 cup bundt tin with a little vegetable oil and dust the inside with the breadcrumbs or plain flour. Transfer the dough to the prepared tin and make sure the top is even and smooth. Cover again with a cloth and leave to prove in a warm place for another 30 minutes.

Meanwhile, preheat your oven to 180°C/160°C Fan/Gas Mark 4/350°F.

Bake the bundt in the centre of the oven for 35 minutes. Leave to cool in the tin before turning it out onto a serving plate.

Mix the water into the icing sugar to make a glaze. You can tint this with a little natural food colouring, if you like. Drizzle the icing over your bundt and serve.

ST. MARTIN'S CROISSANTS WITH ALMOND PASTE

The St. Martin's croissant, or *rogal świętomarciński*, is said to have existed in Poznań, Poland, since 1860, and it is traditionally baked and eaten on 11 November. The old town of Poznań is a truly fascinating place to visit, and lying 50km to the west is Gniezno, widely thought to have been the first capital of Poland. If you are considering a historical trip to the legendary land of '*Lech, Czech, i Rus*', you must visit both Poznań and Gniezno, picking up a croissant along the way. Making your own croissant dough is a little time-consuming, so I have suggested using a store-bought variety to make these at home. However, if you ever visit Poznań, be sure to pop into the croissant museum in the old town to learn how the traditional recipe, which is protected, was made. The filling is made with white poppy seeds, vanilla, dates or figs, raisins and cream. The legend states that a baker in Poznań had a dream about St. Martin, who rode by on his horse and lost a horseshoe, hence, the shape of the croissant. White poppy seeds can be widely found online.

Makes 12

2 x 350g packs of store-bought croissant dough

a little milk, for glazing

2 tbsp water

50g icing sugar

50g flaked almonds, lightly toasted in a dry pan

For the paste:

100g white poppy seeds

200g ground almonds (or use almonds and any mixed nuts)

200g icing sugar

100ml double cream

grated zest of ½ orange

100g raisins, soaked in a little hot tea and strained (or try stoned dates or dried figs)

To make the paste, rinse the poppy seeds in a bowl of cold water and drain. Cover them with boiling water and leave for 30 minutes.

Strain off any excess water from the poppy seeds, then transfer them to a high-powered blender and pulse. Add the ground almonds, icing sugar, double cream and orange zest, then pulse until you have a thick paste. Stir in the raisins, if using. If you are using dates or dried figs, you can blend them with the rest of the ingredients.

Preheat your oven to 200°C/180°C Fan/Gas Mark 6/400°F. Line a large baking tray with baking paper.

Use a sharp knife to separate your croissant dough into triangles where they are marked out. Place 2 teaspoons of the poppy seed paste along the longest edge of each triangle. Starting from that longest edge, roll up the croissant quite tightly, then curl up the edges slightly to form more of a U shape. Place on the lined baking tray, leaving a little room between each one. Brush with a little milk, then bake in the oven for 10–15 minutes, or until the croissants have risen and are golden. Remove from the oven and leave to cool slightly on a wire rack.

Make the icing by the water into the icing sugar. Drizzle the icing over each croissant and top with lightly toasted almonds. Serve warm.

POPPY SEED CINNAMON BUNS WITH CREAM CHEESE GLAZE

Over the years, I have experimented with making a traditional *makowiec*, or poppy seed roll, but recently I experimented with a more modern cinnamon bun recipe, adding poppy seed paste and a drizzle of melted-down Polish fudge, or *krówki*, but you can also use any caramel sauce. You can either arrange the buns in a deep baking tin, as you would cinnamon rolls, or chop the dough into bigger pieces (around 7.5cm/3in wide), then use the handle of a wooden spoon to gently press down lengthways across the middle of the dough and bake them as individual buns. You'll need to pop to the Polish shop to buy a can of poppy seed paste, or you can make your own following the instructions in Baking Basics on page 24.

Makes 15

375g strong white bread flour, plus an extra 50g if needed, plus extra for dusting

100g caster sugar

14g fresh yeast, crumbled (or 7g instant dried yeast)

200ml lukewarm milk

2 eggs, beaten

75g butter, melted

1 tsp vanilla bean paste

a pinch of salt

1 tsp vegetable oil

For the filling:

60g butter, melted

1 x quantity of Poppy Seed Paste (see page 24) or 350g canned masa makowa

2 tsp ground cinnamon

200g soft light brown sugar

4 tbsp Caramel Sauce (see p28)

For the glaze:

50g icing sugar

50g cream cheese or twaróg sernikowy (see page 20)

2 tbsp milk

continued over-leaf

Put 1 tablespoon of the flour, 1 tablespoon of the sugar and the yeast in a bowl, stir in a little of the lukewarm milk and whisk until you have a thick paste. Leave in a warm place for 10 minutes.

In a stand mixer fitted with a dough hook, or in a bowl, combine the rest of the sugar and milk, the eggs, melted butter and vanilla, and mix well. Add the yeast mixture and mix again, then sift in the remaining 375g (minus the 1 tablespoon) of flour and a pinch of salt. Knead the dough (using the dough hook or start with a wooden spoon and then knead by hand) for 8–10 minutes. The dough should have formed a ball. If it has not, add the 50g of additional flour. Grease a separate, clean bowl with some of the vegetable oil and transfer your ball of dough to the bowl. Cover with a clean cloth and leave to prove in a warm place for at least 1 hour.

Once your dough has risen, tip it out onto a board sprinkled with flour and knead for a minute until you knock most of the air out, then refrigerate for up to 30 minutes to make it easier to roll.

Dust the board with a little more flour and roll the dough out into a rectangle shape, roughly 30 x 20cm/12 x 8in. Brush your melted butter for

the filling all over the dough, leaving a 3cm/1 ¼ in border, then spread over the poppy seed paste. Sprinkle over the cinnamon and sugar, as evenly as possible, then drizzle over the caramel sauce. Starting with the longest edge, roll the dough up into a tight roll. Trim the edges and cut into 15 equal pieces.

Grease and line a 30 x 23cm/12 x 9in rectangular baking tin with a little oil and a sheet of baking paper. Place the buns cut-side up in the lined tin so that you can see the swirls. The tin should fit 5 buns across and 3 down. Cover with a clean cloth and leave to prove in a warm place for 1 hour.

Preheat your oven to 180°C/160°C Fan/Gas Mark 4/350°F.

Bake in the centre of the oven for 20 minutes, or until the buns are light golden on top. If they are not quite golden, keep them in for another 5 minutes.

Cool slightly in tin before removing to a wire rack. To make the glaze, whisk the icing sugar with the cream cheese and milk until you have a thick paste. Spread the glaze over the buns, and eat them while they are warm.

SEROMAKOWIEC

Cheesecake with Poppy Seed Paste

Polish baking so often incorporates poppy seeds, especially on the festive table, when the poppy seed roll *makowiec* makes a star appearance, as do noodles with poppy seeds. This is because poppy seeds are associated with prosperity, happiness and even fertility according to Eastern European tradition. This is a recipe for a cheesecake marbled with a poppy seed paste. It's quite nice in place of making a poppy seed roll, which can take a bit of effort. You can buy the paste in cans from a Polish supermarket, or you can make your own paste (see Baking Basics on page 24). For a deeper cake, you can also bake this in a square tin.

Serves 12

400g Poppy Seed Paste (see
   Baking Basics, page 24) or ½ x
   850g can of masa makowa

100g butter, at room temperature,
   plus extra for greasing

100g caster sugar

2 eggs

1 tsp vanilla bean paste

400g cream cheese or twaróg
   sernikowy (see page 20)

100ml sour cream

75ml double cream

45g cornflour or potato flour

icing sugar, for dusting

If you have made your own poppy seed paste, take it out of the refrigerator and let it come to room temperature. If you are using canned paste, transfer it to a bowl and leave it at room temperature.

Preheat your oven to 170°C/150°C Fan/Gas Mark 3½/340°F. Grease and line a 30 x 23cm/12 x 9in rectangular baking tin, about 5cm/2in deep, with butter and baking paper.

In a clean bowl or a stand mixer, beat the caster sugar and butter together for a few minutes. Add the eggs, one by one, and beat again, followed by the vanilla bean paste. Beat in the cream cheese, then the sour cream. Pour in the double cream and beat again until slightly thickened. Stir in the cornflour or potato flour until fully incorporated.

Spread half of the poppy seed paste over the bottom of the lined tin, then pour in the cheesecake batter. Use a tablespoon to drop small amounts of the remaining poppy seed paste all over the cheesecake batter, then use a knife to carefully swirl the paste into the mixture to create a pattern.

Prepare a bain marie by filling a large, shallow roasting tin three-quarters full with hot water. Place your cheesecake tin into the hot water, then transfer it to the oven. Bake for 55 minutes–1 hour. It is ready when the sides are firm but the centre is still a little jiggly. The top should be light golden. Once baked, turn your oven off, open the door slightly and leave the cheesecake inside the oven for 1 hour.

Carefully remove the cheesecake from the oven. Leave to cool, then place it in the refrigerator to chill overnight.

The next day, carefully remove the cheesecake from the tin and remove the baking paper. Dust with icing sugar and cut into slices.

KATARZYNKI

Traditional Gingerbread Cookies

Katarzynki or *pierniczki*, cookie-like gingerbread cakes, featured prominently during my childhood. Almost every Sunday after church, we would go to the Polish Ex-Combatants Club (Polski Dom Kombatantów) in Manchester. After the Second World War, some 150,000 Polish armed forces personell and their families settled in Manchester; my father and his brothers among them. My dad would later meet and employ my grandmother, and then my mum, across the road in his factory, Tadlon Productions. Earlier, in 1949, after numerous community fundraising campaigns, an imposing red brick building, formerly a church, was purchased and became the focal point for so many of us. My mum, who was always leading various committees, would rally her own troops and host fundraising events there for the Polish School, or for the Polish Divine Mercy Church. On Sundays, it was my indoor playground, with long corridors, secret hiding places, a restaurant serving endless plates of *pieorgi*, a bar, a library, a snooker room and 10p Space Invader arcade machines. We took part in plays, recitals and concerts on the big stage, often dressed in Polish national costumes. Each Sunday, I would be given a few coins and I'd creep up to the bar to buy a packet of *katarzynki*. I'd sneak away and unwrap the squeaky cellophane wrapping before sinking my teeth into the little spiced cakes, coated in dark chocolate. Sadly, the building was lost to developers, but our memories live on. To make *katarzynki* to their traditional shape, you'll need a cookie cutter called a *foremka do ciasta katarzynka*, but you could also make rectangular shapes or heart-shaped cookies. It is said that the Polish *katarzynka* originated in Toruń, a medieval town in Poland, known as the birthplace of Nicolaus Copernicus and famous for artisan gingerbread. The original recipe, dating back to 1380, is a closely guarded secret, but it contained honey, flour (a rye-wheat blend) and spices.

Makes 20

200g runny honey

100g soft dark brown sugar

100g butter, at room temperature

100g white rye flour

300g plain flour, plus extra for
    dusting

1 tsp baking powder

1 tsp bicarbonate of soda

2 tsp ground cinnamon

1 tsp ground cloves

1 tsp ground allspice

2 tsp cocoa powder

2 egg yolks

400g good-quality dark
    chocolate, melted

Put the honey, sugar and butter into a small pan, whisk together and heat gently until melted. Set aside.

Combine the dry ingredients in a large bowl, along with the egg yolks. Mix together, then pour in the melted liquid. Keep mixing until a dough forms. Cover with clingfilm and chill in the refrigerator for 1 hour.

Preheat your oven to 180°C/160°C Fan/Gas Mark 4/350°F. Line a baking sheet with baking paper.

Sprinkle a board with a little flour and roll out the dough (it's easier if you roll it out between two sheets of baking paper). Using a cookie cutter, cut into shapes and place them carefully onto the lined baking sheet, leaving at least 1cm/½in between each cookie.

Bake (in batches if needed) for 20 minutes, or until the cookies are light golden on top. They will puff up slightly and they will harden. They need to soften a little, so cool completely on a wire rack, then transfer them to a tin to mature for 2 weeks, before coating with chocolate.

To coat, place the cookies on a wire rack and spoon the melted chocolate over them Once dry, store them in a tin.

CHRISTMAS COOKIE 'LETTERS' TO ST. NICHOLAS

Every year, the children and I make a big batch of spiced Christmas cookies, some to give away and some to hang up on the tree. They seemed to be one of the most popular recipes in my previous book, *Wild Honey and Rye*. These are a simpler version of cookie 'letters', as in the letters that you might write to Father Christmas or St. Nicholas (*Święty Mikołaj*) who comes a little earlier in Poland, on 6 December, to bring gifts. If you cut these with a fluted or scalloped-edged rectangular cookie cutter, they will look a little more like letters or envelopes.

Makes about 20

115g butter, plus extra for greasing

115g soft dark brown sugar

8 tbsp runny honey

250g plain flour, plus extra for dusting

200g white rye flour

2 tsp baking powder

2 tsp ground ginger

2 tsp ground cinnamon

2 tsp allspice

2 tbsp cocoa powder

1 egg

To decorate:

50g icing sugar

1–2 tbsp water

Preheat your oven to 200°C/180°C Fan/400°F/Gas Mark 6. Lightly grease two large baking sheets with butter.

Put the butter, brown sugar and honey in a small saucepan over a gentle heat. Stir only until the butter has melted. Set aside.

In a large bowl, sift the dry ingredients together, mix well, add the egg and mix again. Pour the melted butter mixture into the dry ingredients and stir until the dough starts to come together.

Tip the mixture out onto a lightly floured work surface and knead to form a ball. If the mixture is too crumbly, add a tablespoon of water at a time and knead again until it comes together. Roll out the dough to about 3mm/1/8in thick. Cut out rectangles, using a scalloped rectangular cookie cutter, and carefully lift the cookies onto the lined baking sheets (leave space around each cookie).

Bake in the oven for 7–8 minutes per batch, until golden. When the cookies are baked, they will still be a bit soft. Using a palette knife, carefully lift them onto a wire rack and leave to cool.

While the cookies are baking, make the icing by stirring together the icing sugar and water. Fill a piping bag fitted with a fine plain nozzle with the icing and set aside.

For the decoration, pipe a line of icing around the edge of each rectanglecookie . Then, make a dot of icing in the centre of the rectangle and pipe a line from the top left corner of the rectangle to the centre dot, then from the top right corner of the rectangle to the dot, to form the V-shape of the envelope. Leave to set before serving.

CHOCOLATE GINGERBREAD CAKE WITH PLUM SYRUP

Alongside the gingerbread cookies and the poppy seed cakes, you'll usually find a traditional gingerbread cake, layered with plum jam, on the Christmas table. To make life very simple at the busiest time of year, I've perfected a chocolate gingerbread cake that almost anyone will be able to pull off. The plum syrup can be made in advance (and if you make an extra batch, a plum vodka cocktail is equally simple to throw together).

Serves 8

200g butter, at room temperature
  (plus extra, for greasing)
180g soft dark brown sugar
300g runny honey
2 eggs
300g self-raising flour
1 tsp bicarbonate of soda
50g cocoa powder
2 tsp ground ginger
2 tsp ground cinnamon
1 tbsp allspice
100g good-quality dark chocolate,
  grated, or chocolate chips
125ml freshly brewed hot coffee

For the plum syrup:

6 plums, halved and stoned
125g caster sugar
200ml water
1 x quantity of Chocolate Glaze
  (see Baking Basics, page 28)
chopped hazelnuts or almonds,
  to decorate

Preheat your oven to 180°C/160°C Fan/Gas Mark 4/350°F. Grease and line a 30 x 23cm/12 x 9in rectangular baking tin, about 5cm/2in deep, with butter and baking paper.

Place all the ingredients for the gingerbread cake into a food processor (pouring the coffee in last) and pulse until everything comes together.

Pour the batter into your lined tin and bake in the centre of the oven for 35–40 minutes, or until a skewer inserted into the middle of the cake comes out clean. Leave it to cool in the tin.

For the plum syrup, place the plums in a pan with the caster sugar and water. Bring to the boil, then simmer, uncovered, until the plums soften and a syrup forms. Leave in the pan to cool, then drain the syrup through a sieve, pushing all the juice out of the plums with the back of a spoon. You should have around 125ml of plum syrup. You could spoon the leftover plum pulp over some yoghurt for breakfast.

Make some holes in the top of the cake and drizzle the plum syrup over the top.

Make the chocolate glaze according to the instructions on page 28 and pour it evenly over the cake.

Leave to set for five minuted, then remove the cake from the tin and serve on a larger platter, decorated with a few chopped hazelnuts or almonds.

Easter, Christmas and Other Occasions

ORANGE SHORTBREAD STARS

Like the gingerbread 'envelopes' or 'letters' (on page 122), these orange shortbread stars are a lovely Christmas project to bake with children.

Makes 16–20

For the shortbread:

200g plain flour, plus extra for dusting

100g ground almonds

100g caster sugar

125g butter, at room temperature

a pinch of salt

1 egg

1 tsp orange extract

grated zest of 1 orange

For the icing:

100g icing sugar

2 tbsp orange juice

sprinkles or chopped candied fruit, to decorate

Tip all the shortbread ingredients into a food processor and pulse until a ball of dough forms. Alternatively, bring everything together by hand in a large bowl. Wrap the dough in clingfilm and chill in the refrigerator for 1 hour.

Preheat your oven to 180°C/160°C Fan/Gas Mark 4/350°F. Line a large baking tray wth baking paper.

Cut the dough in half and roll each out on a board sprinkled with flour. You might find it easier to roll the dough out between two sheets of baking paper. Cut out star shapes with a cookie cutter, approximately 7cm in diameter, and carefully lift them onto the lined baking tray.

Bake (in batches, if needed) in the oven for 10 minutes until golden. Transfer the cookies to a wire rack and leave to cool completely.

For the icing, mix the icing sugar with the orange juice until a smooth paste forms. Spread this over the cookies and decorate with the sprinkles or chopped candied fruit. Leave the icing to set completely before serving.

PANCAKES AND PIEROGI

NALEŚNIKI

Pancakes Three Ways

Polish pancakes, or crêpes, are called *naleśniki* and they can be filled with a variety of fillings. They are generally eaten as a late-afternoon snack, rather than on a specific day. Traditionally, they are filled either with warmed, stewed apples or with sweetened cream cheese. They can also be filled and baked in a buttered dish (with an extra bit of butter on top of each pancake) at 180°C/160°C Fan/Gas Mark 4/350°F for 15 minutes. The filling (sweet cream cheese or apple) is enough to fill 6 pancakes, so you would have to make double to fill 12 pancakes with one filling. For a simple alternative, try apricot jam/preserve with a drizzle of melted chocolate.

Makes 12

125g plain flour
2 eggs
250ml milk
40g butter, melted
1 tsp vanilla bean paste
a pinch of salt
vegetable oil, for frying
icing sugar, to finish

For a sweet cream cheese filling:

200g cream cheese or twaróg
  *sernikowy (see page 20), at
  room temperature*
2 tbsp caster sugar
1 tsp vanilla bean paste
*2 tbsp raisins, soaked in a little
  hot tea*

For an apricot jam filling:

*Apricot Jam (see Quince or Apricot
  Jam with Tea, page 174)*
*50g good-quality milk or dark
  chocolate, melted*

For a stewed apple filling:

*150g warm Stewed Apples (see
  Baking Basics, page 25)*

Whisk the flour, eggs, milk, melted butter, vanilla and salt together in a jug until the batter is smooth. This benefits from a rest in the refrigerator for 30 minutes.

For the cream cheese filling, mix together the cream cheese, sugar and vanilla until smooth. Drain the raisins and stir them in. Chill until needed.

For the pancakes, heat a shallow frying pan or a pancake pan over a medium heat. Drizzle a little oil into the pan, then use a piece of kitchen paper to gently wipe away any excess. Pour a ladleful of the pancake batter into the pan, swirl it round and cook on one side for 2–3 minutes. Flip the pancake over and cook the other side for 2 minutes more, then transfer the cooked pancake to a waiting plate and keep warm. Brush the pan with a little more oil and repeat with the remaining batter to make 12 pancakes in total.

Fill the hot pancakes with your preferred selection of fillings and dust with icing sugar. If filling with apricot preserve, drizzle the pancakes with a little melted chocolate before serving.

RACUCHY

Pancake Fritters with Stewed Apples and Honey-Roasted Plums

My children devour these whenever my Mama makes them. They are a childhood favourite in most Polish kitchens. They make everything better. I would normally peel and core a few apples to make these, and stir the pieces through the batter, but recently Mama had a jar of stewed apples and she dropped a tablespoon of them onto each pancake while frying. The variation was a good one. To turn these into more of a dessert, serve them with honey-roasted plums, a dollop of whipped cream and perhaps a dusting of ground cinnamon.

Makes 12

2 eggs, beaten

125g self-raising flour

250ml milk

2 tbsp caster sugar

2 tsp ground cinnamon

a pinch of salt

2 tbsp sour cream or natural yogurt

2 tbsp vegetable oil, or as needed, for frying

icing sugar or ground cinnamon, for dusting

whipped cream, to serve

For the stewed apples:

3 eating apples, peeled, cored and cubed

1 tbsp lemon juice

3 tbsp caster sugar or soft light brown sugar

1 tsp ground cinnamon

2 tbsp water

For the honey-roasted plums:

6 plums, halved and stoned

3 tbsp soft light brown sugar

a generous drizzle of runny honey

Make the stewed apples first. Put the apples, lemon juice, sugar and cinnamon into a pan, add the water, cover with a lid and cook over a low heat for 5–7 minutes. Set aside to cool.

If serving with the roasted plums, preheat your oven to 200°C/180°C Fan/Gas Mark 6/400°F. Place the plums, cut-side up, on a baking tray lined with baking paper, sprinkle over the sugar and drizzle with honey. Bake in the oven for 30–40 minutes, or until soft.

For the pancake fritters, put the eggs into a bowl with the flour, milk, sugar, cinnamon, salt and sour cream or yogurt. Whisk everything together until you have a smooth batter.

Heat the oil in a large, wide frying pan over a medium heat. Using a large tablespoon, spoon some of the batter in to the pan to form an American-style pancake. Place 1 tablespoon of the stewed apple into the centre, then top with a little more batter. Repeat to make two other pancake fritters in the pan. Fry on one side for 1–2 minutes until golden, then carefully flip each pancake fritter over and continue cooking for 1–2 minutes on the other side. Transfer the pancake fritters to a plate lined with kitchen paper once fried. Add a little more oil to the pan each time and fry the pancake fritters in batches of three at a time, so that you don't overcrowd the pan.

Serve the pancake fritters with a dusting of icing sugar and eat straight away, or serve them with the roasted plums, whipped cream and a sprinkling of cinnamon for an extra treat.

TORT NALEŚNIKOWY

Crêpe Cake with Caramel Sauce and Sesame Snaps

This caramel crêpe cake is a great alternative to baking a cake for a special occasion, especially as the pancakes can be made in advance and warmed up just before serving. The filling is inspired by the 'sesame snaps' of my childhood, another Polish snack, or treat, called *sezamki*. These are sesame snap biscuits, which are widely available.

Serves 12

2 x quantity of Naleśniki Pancakes
(see page 128)

2 x quantity of Caramel Sauce (see
Baking Basics, page 28) or a
600g jar of good-quality caramel
sauce

4 x 30g packets of 'sesame snap'
biscuits

For the cream filling:

500g mascarpone cheese

300ml double cream

3 tbsp runny honey

1 tsp vanilla bean paste

Make two batches of pancakes, so that you have 24 pancakes in total. To warm them up before serving, stack them on a plate, cover with foil and warm them in ta preheated oven at 180°C/160°C Fan/Gas Mark 4/350°F for 10 minutes.

Make your caramel sauce, or warm up the store-bought caramel sauce in a small pan.

For the cream filling, mix together the mascarpone, double cream, honey and vanilla until combined.

You can make all of this in advance, but make sure the caramel is warm and that the mascarpone mixture is at room temperature before assembling.

Crumble, bash or blitz in a food processor, three packets of sesame snap biscuits, reserving the fourth packet for decorating the top layer.

To assemble the cake, place one pancake on a serving plate, spread 2–3 tablespoons of the cream filling evenly over the pancake, then put another pancake on top, spread over 2–3 tablespoons of caramel sauce and sprinkle over some of the crushed sesame snaps. Keep alternating layers like this until you have used up all the pancakes. Decorate the top with the remaining cream filling, a drizzle of caramel sauce, the fourth packet of sesame snap biscuits, broken into shards/pieces, and any remaining crumbs.

EASY FRUIT-FILLED PIEROGI

Pierogi can be filled with a variety of fruit, most commonly with blueberries when in season, or with strawberries, or pitted cherries. However, sweet plums, stoned and chopped, also make a delicious filling. In all cases, you can boil the *pierogi*, then pan-fry gently in a little unsalted butter so they become a little crispy. For an extra treat, although not traditional, add a square of milk chocolate to the fruit inside before cooking.

Makes about 20

350g plain flour or '00' pasta flour, plus extra for dusting

1 tbsp icing sugar, plus extra for dusting

1 egg, plus 1 egg yolk

125ml lukewarm water

1 tbsp vegetable oil

For the fruit filling:

1kg fruit, such as chopped strawberries, whole blueberries or plums or apricots, stoned and chopped

1 tbsp caster sugar

To serve:

icing sugar, for dusting

a little melted butter

sour cream, sweetened with a little honey

Mix the flour with the icing sugar until combined, then add the egg and egg yolk and stir with a knife. Slowly add the lukewarm water and oil, mixing until a dough starts to form.

Tip the dough onto a lightly floured board and knead for about 5 minutes, just until the mixture comes together with no lumps and feels smooth. Wrap the dough in clingfilm and leave it to rest for at least 30 minutes in the refrigerator.

To make the fruit filling, wash your fruit, place it into a large bowl and sprinkle over the sugar. Leave this to sit for fifteen minutes, just until the sugar dissolves.

Meanwhile, bring a large pan of water to a rolling boil. Roll out your dough on a board dusted with a little icing plain flour. You are aiming for the dough to be around 3mm/1/8in thick. Use a 9cm/3½in pastry cutter or a glass tumbler to cut out circles of dough.

Take your fruit filling, drain away any sugar syrup, and place a tablespoon of filling onto each circle. Working quite quickly, take each circle in your hand, fold the dough over to form a semicircle and pinch the dough along the edge so that each dumpling is well sealed. Place each one back on the board dusted with flour sugar. Cover with a tea towel while you make the rest.

To cook the dumplings, carefully drop them into the boiling water, in batches of 5 at a time, until each one floats to the surface. They will only take a minute or so to cook. Carefully remove each one with a slotted spoon and plate on a large platter.

Serve with a dusting of icing sugar, a drizzle of melted butter and some sweetened sour cream.

PIEROGI WITH SWEET CREAM CHEESE

My favourite savoury *pierogi* (Polish folded dumplings) are ones filled generously with mashed potato and cheese, but sometimes it's a nice alternative to make *pierogi* with a sweet filling. The sweet cream cheese theme is strong in the Polish kitchen, influenced by *sernik*, or Polish cheesecake – so these are *pierogi ze serem na słodko*. A variation of these might be the pancakes with raisins and sweet cream cheese on page 128. The filling here needs to be very cold/straight from the refrigerator, because you have to be able to fold the dumplings easily to enclose the filling and you don't want the filling to escape while they are boiling. They should be served with a respectable amount of thick and slightly sweetened sour cream on the side.

Makes about 20

350g plain flour or '00' pasta flour,
  plus extra for dusting

1 tbsp icing sugar, plus extra for
  dusting

1 egg, plus 1 egg yolk

125ml lukewarm water

1 tbsp vegetable oil

For the sweet cream cheese
  filling:

750g cream cheese or twaróg
  sernikowy (see page 20)

2 egg yolks

3 tbsp caster sugar

1 tsp vanilla bean paste

To serve:

icing sugar, for dusting

a little melted butter

sour cream, sweetened with
  a little runny honey

Mix the flour with the icing sugar until combined, then add the egg and egg yolk and stir with a knife. Slowly add the lukewarm water and oil, mixing until a dough starts to form.

Tip the dough onto a lightly floured board and knead for about 5 minutes, just until the mixture comes together with no lumps and feels smooth. Wrap the dough in clingfilm and leave it to rest for at least 30 minutes in the refrigerator.

For the sweet cream cheese filling, mix all the ingredients together until well combined, then chill in the refrigerator, too, for an hour.

When you are ready to make the *pierogi*, bring a large pan of water to a rolling boil.

Roll out your dough on a board dusted with a little icing sugar. You are aiming for the dough to be around 3mm/⅛in thick. Use a 9cm/3½in pastry cutter or a glass tumbler to cut out circles of dough. Take your cheese filling out of the refrigerator and place a tablespoon of filling onto each circle. Working quite quickly, take each circle in your hand, fold the dough over to form a semi-circle and pinch the dough along the edge so that each dumpling is well sealed. Place each one back on the board dusted with icing sugar.

To cook the dumplings, carefully drop them into the boiling water, in batches of five at a time, until each one floats to the surface. They will only take a minute or so to cook. Carefully remove each one with a slotted spoon and place on a large platter.

Serve with a dusting of icing sugar, a drizzle of melted butter and some sweetened sour cream.

LAZY DUMPLINGS WITH FRUIT, CINNAMON AND CREAM

Leniwe in Polish means 'lazy', and it is one of my favourite words. The Poles love *kluski,* or dumplings, sometimes known as *pierogi leniwe,* doused in melted butter, sprinkled with sugar and cinnamon and usually served with cream. Occasionally, you'll see them sprinkled with fried breadcrumbs, too. If you serve these with berries, or even a fruit compote, you get a simpler-to-make version of fruit-filled *pierogi,* and you don't have to stand for hours folding and sticking. This dish provides such a good hit of comfort that you'll need a blanket and a lie down afterwards. Again, they are made with *twaróg,* or curd cheese, but you can use any type of cream cheese for these.

Serves 4

For the dumplings:

250g full-fat cream cheese or twaróg sernikowy *(see page 20)* or curd cheese

1 egg

1 tbsp cornflour or potato flour

125g plain flour, plus extra for dusting

To serve:

125g butter

2–3 tbsp caster sugar

1 tsp ground cinnamon

2–3 tbsp fresh white breadcrumbs *(optional)*

200g forest fruits, blueberries or pitted cherries (fresh, or frozen, defrosted)

whipped cream or double cream

Mix all the ingredients for the dumplings together in a bowl or a stand mixer until a soft dough forms. Tip the dough onto a board dusted with flour and bring it together into a ball. If the dough is too sticky, add a little more flour, but not too much. Cut the dough into quarters and roll each piece into a long cylinder. Flatten slightly, then cut the dough at an angle into 2.5cm/1in pieces.

Bring a large pan of water to a rapid boil. Drop the dumplings into the boiling water (you can do this in two batches). As soon as they come to the surface, take them out with a slotted spoon and place them on a large plate. This should take 3–4 minutes per batch.

In a separate pan, melt the butter, then add 1–2 tablespoons of the sugar and the ground cinnamon. If using breadcrumbs, toast them in the butter and sugar until golden brown.

Scatter the fruit over the dumplings and sprinkle with 1 tablespoon of sugar. Drizzle the butter, or buttery breadcrumbs, over the dumplings and fruit. Serve with whipped cream or double cream.

KNEDLE

Plum-Apricot Dumplings with Brown Butter Sugar and Cinnamon

We're travelling back to the Austro-Hungarian Empire with this recipe, as *knedle*, a type of dumpling made with potatoes and flour, are a version of the German *knödel*, a boiled dumpling. These are generally a savoury dish, or a side dish, but there are dessert versions made with plums and, in season, sometimes apricots and other fruit. These are very popular in Austria, too, and in other central European countries. They are actually very easy to make, because the dough, made from potatoes, is very forgiving and is shaped into a ball around a piece, or pieces, of fruit. Unlike *pierogi*, these don't have to be perfect and they certainly don't have to look pretty – they simply exist to satisfy a doughy-dumplingy comfort food craving every now and again. If I have leftover mashed potatoes, I either make these or *kopytka* ('little hooves'), both of which can be served with a nutty butter drizzle and buttery cinnamon breadcrumbs and cream. Even though they can be made with summer fruits, such as strawberries, I prefer the autumnal cold-weather angle. There's a certain robustness about these that my Babcia Tekla appreciated very much.

Makes 12

8–10 potatoes, peeled, cooked and mashed, then left until cold (or around 250g cold mashed potatoes – enough to fill 2 x 240ml cups)

250g plain flour, plus extra for dusting

1 egg

1 tbsp cream cheese or twaróg sernikowy (see page 20) (optional)

12 plums or apricots (or 6 of each), halved and stoned

To serve:

3 tbsp butter

3 tbsp soft light brown sugar

1 tsp ground cinnamon

double cream

To make the dumpling dough, mix together the mashed potato, flour, egg and cream cheese in a bowl by hand. Sprinkle a large board with flour and divide the dough into 12 equal portions. Flatten each piece of dough with the palm of your hand, so that you have rough circle shapes. Place two plum or two apricot halves together to form their original shape (minus the stone) and place in the centre of a circle of dough. Form the dough into a ball to enclose it. Repeat until all are filled.

Fill a large pan with water and bring to the boil. Working with 3–4 dumplings at a time, gently lower them into the water and simmer over a very gentle heat for around 10 minutes per batch. Carefully remove each dumpling and place it on a platter.

Meanwhile, prepare the topping to serve by melting the butter in a frying pan over a medium heat until dark, golden and a nutty brown colour. Add the sugar to the pan and let it sizzle a little, then sprinkle in the cinnamon.

Serve the dumplings, sprinkled with the brown butter sugar and a generous lashing of double cream. Eat immediately.

GLUTEN-FREE CHOCOLATE AND COCONUT PANCAKES GF

These are a tasty alternative when looking for a gluten-free treat. While coconut might have been seen as an exotic ingredient in Poland's past, alternative milks, flours and sweeteners are now mainstream and find themselves blended into many recipes. The chocolate chips studded inside the pancakes go particularly well with the Honey-Roasted Plums from the *Racuchy* recipe on page 130. These are slightly thicker, American-style pancakes.

Makes 12

150ml coconut milk or coconut cream (from a can – not coconut water)

2 eggs, plus 1 egg white

40g butter, melted

3 tbsp runny honey

200g gluten-free self-raising flour

100g dark, milk or white chocolate chips

vegetable oil, for frying

50g desiccated coconut, slightly toasted

fresh fruit of your choice, to serve (or serve with the Honey-Roasted Plums from page 130)

Mix the coconut milk or coconut cream with the whole eggs, melted butter and honey. Stir through the flour until there are no lumps. Chill in the refrigerator for up to 2 hours.

When you are ready to make the pancakes, whisk the egg white to soft peaks and stir it into the batter, followed by the chocolate chips.

Heat a large, non-stick frying pan over a medium heat and drizzle in a little oil. Add a ladleful of pancake batter to the pan – the pancake should fluff up and little air bubbles will start to appear. Using a spatula, carefully flip the pancake over until the other side cooks through. Transfer the pancake to a plate and keep warm before repeating with all the remaining batter, adding a little extra oil periodically.

Serve the warm pancakes sprinkled with toasted coconut and topped with fresh fruit.

PLACKI

Potato Pancakes with Cream and Sugar

These potato pancakes are a staple teatime treat, often just a savoury snack (with a little grated onion), but we like them best with the addition of a bit of grated apple and then sprinkled with sugar and cream. You could experiment with a little grated courgette, but if you are serving them sweet, with sugar and cream, still add the apple. If you grate the potatoes using a box grater on the larger holes, the result is a pancake that is coarser, perhaps a little crisper when fried, like a *latke* (a Jewish potato pancake), but my family's way is to grate the potato very finely, so the mixture is softer. If you only have a large grater, you can also whizz the mixture in a food processor to achieve the same result. To bind, I use cornflour, or rice flour, so they are also gluten-free. These are also nice with sugar and sour cream, instead of double cream.

Makes 12

4 large or 8 medium potatoes
1 eating apple
1 egg, beaten
2 tbsp cornflour or rice flour
a pinch of salt
vegetable oil, for frying

To serve:
granulated sugar
double cream or sour cream

Peel and grate the potatoes and the apple into a bowl. Add the egg, cornflour or rice, flour and a pinch of salt, and stir. Quickly pulse half of the mixture in a food processor and then add back into the grated mixture to achieve a slightly smoother batter.

Heat a frying pan with a good 1cm/½in depth of oil over a medium heat. Spoon in 2–3 tablespoons of the potato batter for each pancake. Fry on one side until golden brown, then flip over and fry gently on the other side. Remove the pancake with a slotted spatula to a plate lined with kitchen paper and keep warm. Repeat until all the batter is used up, adding a little extra oil periodically.

To serve, sprinkle generously with granulated sugar and pour over a generous amount of double cream or sour cream.

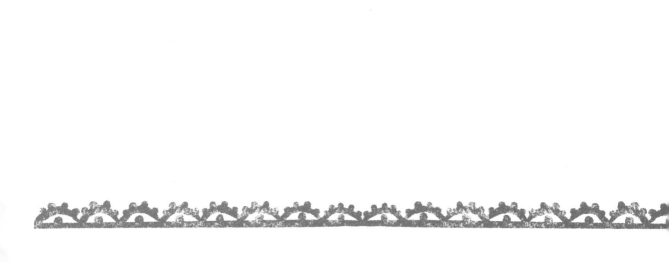

BREAD, LOAVES AND BUNS

FLUFFY BREAKFAST BUNS

These little buns are easy to make. They are a cross between a bun and a bagel, because you drop them into boiling water before baking. These are best served warm, gently pulled apart, with a thick layer of a thick fruit jam. Even if you are not a baker, these home-made buns are worth a try.

Makes 8

500g strong white bread flour, plus extra for dusting

30g fresh yeast, crumbled (or 10g fast-action dried yeast)

1 tbsp caster sugar

350ml lukewarm water

4 tbsp butter, melted

1 tsp salt

To finish:

3 tsp bicarbonate of soda

1 tsp salt

1 egg yolk, beaten

2–3 tbsp mixed poppy seeds and sesame seeds

In a jug, combine 2 tablespoons of the flour with the yeast, sugar and half of the lukewarm water. Gently stir, then set aside in a warm place for 15 minutes.

Sift the remaining flour into a large bowl, then add the yeast mixture along with the rest of the water. Add the melted butter and the salt, and bring the mixture together. You can either do this by hand, or with a stand mixer fitted with a dough hook. Knead for 5 minutes until the dough is soft and elastic. Cover with a clean cloth and leave in a warm place for 1 hour. The dough should more or less double in size.

Line a baking tray with paper paper. Tip the dough onto a surface lightly dusted with flour and cut into eight portions. Form into little balls and flatten them slightly, then place them on the lined baking tray. Cover the buns with a cloth and leave them in a warm place for a further 15–20 minutes.

Preheat your oven to 190°C/170°C Fan/Gas Mark 5/375°F.

Bring a large pan of water (about 2 litres) to the boil. Add the bicarbonate of soda and salt. Drop in 2–3 buns at a time and cook for 30 seconds, flipping them over halfway through. Remove with a slotted spoon to the baking tray lined with baking paper.

Brush each bun with the beaten egg yolk and sprinkle with the mixed poppy and sesame seeds. Bake in the centre of the oven for 15–20 minutes until the buns are golden brown. Leave to cool on a wire rack for a little while before serving.

Serve the warm buns with unsalted butter and fruit jam, or with any savoury fillings of your choice.

SWEET ONION AND POPPY SEED ROLLS

This is, again, perhaps veering on savoury, but these sweet onion buns make a lovely breakfast treat, alongside scrambled eggs and some fresh fruit. I make mine with very sweet caramelised onions, and the dough is soft and pillowy. These are reminiscent of the *cebularz Lubelski*, a sweet onion bun originating from Lublin, where my paternal grandparents hailed from. Much like the *babka* loaf, these sweet onion buns likely have Jewish roots.

Makes 12

500g plain flour, plus extra for dusting

14g instant dried yeast

1 tbsp caster sugar

250ml lukewarm milk

50g butter, melted

1 egg, plus 1 egg yolk, beaten, for glazing

1 tsp salt

For the sweet onion filling:

3 large white onions (sweet, if you can find them)

2 tbsp vegetable oil

1 tsp butter

1 tbsp caster sugar

50g poppy seeds

First, make the sweet onion filling. Finely chop the onions (or use a food processor to blitz them), then tip them into a large frying pan with the oil and butter. Fry the onions very gently, over a very low heat, for around 10 minutes. They will soften and turn light golden brown – do not let them burn. Once they start turning golden, sprinkle in the sugar and keep frying them for another few minutes, until the sugar melts. Add the poppy seeds and stir, then set aside until completely cold. You can make the onion filling ahead of time.

In a bowl, mix 1 tablespoon of the flour with the yeast, sugar and a little of the lukewarm milk. Whisk and set aside for 10 minutes.

Put the rest of the flour and milk and the melted butter into the bowl of a stand mixer and mix for 2–3 minutes. Switch to a dough hook, add the egg and the salt, and keep mixing until the dough begins to come away from the sides of the bowl. Place a cloth over the bowl and set aside in a wam place for 1–1½ hours.

Line a baking tray with baking paper. Tip the dough out onto a floured board and knead for 2 minutes by hand, then divide the dough into 12 equal pieces. Roll the pieces into balls and place on the lined baking tray. Flatten them slightly with the palm of your hand, then gently make a little dent in the middle of each ball with the back of a tablespoon. Place a large, heaped tablespoon of the onion and poppy seed filling into the middle of each bun. Cover with a clean cloth and leave them to sit for 1 hour.

Preheat your oven to 200°C/180°C Fan/Gas Mark 6/400°F.

Brush the top of each bun (around the filling) with egg yolk. Bake in the oven for 20–25 minutes until the buns are golden on top.

Cool a little on a wire rack. Eat while still warm, served with unsalted butter.

KRAKOWIAN-STYLE BAGELS

If you should ever travel to Krakow, and I would highly recommend it, you'll see a special type of bagel called the *obwarzanek Krakowski*. You won't be able to miss them; they are sold from carts as soon as you hit the arrivals gate at the airport, but more importantly, they are sold by street-traders all across the city from little carts that the traders (some of them in their eighties and beyond) push around while seeking out the best spots from which to sell them. They have been sold across Krakow for over 600 years, and they hold a special PGI status. They are soft and chewy on the inside; a sort of bagel-pretzel hybrid, sprinkled with sesame seeds, poppy seeds or sea salt. These are my take (the original recipe being a closely guarded secret) and, whenever I eat them, I am reminded of my grandfather Anthony, who was born just outside Krakow, and who, I am sure, would have loved the simplicity of these iconic treats. These are best eaten very fresh, so, in Krakow, try and grab one early in the morning. At home, you can treat yourself at any time of the day.

Makes 6

14g fresh yeast, crumbled (or 7g instant dried yeast)

1 tbsp caster sugar

240g plain flour or strong white bread flour, plus extra for dusting

125ml lukewarm milk

1 tsp salt

125ml lukewarm water

2 tbsp vegetable oil, or melted butter, plus extra oil for greasing

1 tsp bicarbonate of soda

1 tbsp runny honey

sesame seeds, poppy seeds, or sea salt, for sprinkling

In a small jug, combine the yeast with the sugar, 1 tablespoon of the flour and the lukewarm milk. Whisk together and leave somewhere warm for 15 minutes.

Pour the yeast mixture into a clean bowl, add the remaining flour, the salt, lukewarm water and vegetable oil or melted butter, and mix everything together well. Knead for around 5–7 minutes. You can also do this in a stand mixer fitted with a dough hook. The dough should come away from the sides of the bowl. Tip the dough out and brush the inside of the bowl with a little oil. Put the dough back in, cover with a clean cloth and leave the dough in a warm place to rest for 30 minutes.

Preheat your oven to 230°C/210°C Fan/Gas Mark 8/450°F. Line two baking trays with baking paper.

Bring a large pan of water to the boil and add the bicarbonate of soda and honey to the water.

Tip the dough out onto a floured board and split into six equal pieces. Roll each piece of dough into a long strip, measuring around 50cm/20in. Fold in half (so you have two strands joined at one end), then twist the two strands together to form a twisted rope. Form into a ring shape and seal the ends together.

Carefully drop each ring into the boiling water, one or two at a time, and blanch them for 30 seconds. Carefully remove with a slotted spoon to the lined baking trays (three on each tray). If the dough has come apart, you can stick it back together at this stage to form a circle again.

Sprinkle the tops with sesame seeds, poppy seeds or sea salt (or a mixture) and bake in the oven for 15 minutes until golden brown on top.

Eat as soon as possible after baking.

CARAWAY ŁOAF

This is a simple loaf, flavoured with caraway seeds, or *kminek,* which is a key flavour in the Polish kitchen, often adding an aromatic note to savoury dishes, such as sauerkraut stew, *bigos,* smoked meats and bread. There is a slight sweetness to this bread and I enjoy it the most when it is still warm, sliced thickly and served with unsalted butter and Polish honey. You can make this loaf as a pure rye loaf, but I often use half rye and half strong white bread flour. You can also make it just with white flour, if you want the caraway to take centre stage.

Makes 1 loaf

14g fresh yeast, crumbled (or 7g
    instant dried yeast)

3 tsp caster sugar

400ml lukewarm water

600g white rye flour (or use strong
    white bread flour, or a mixture),
    plus extra for dusting

a large pinch of salt

50ml vegetable or olive oil, plus
    extra for greasing

4 tsp caraway seeds

2 tsp butter, melted

Put the yeast, sugar and a little of the lukewarm water in a bowl with 1 tablespoon of the flour. Stir and set aside for a few minutes.

Put the rest of the flour into a large bowl or a stand mixer fitted with a dough hook. Add the yeast mixture, the salt, oil, caraway seeds and the rest of the water and mix. Knead for 7–10 minutes, either with the dough hook, or by hand on a board sprinkled with a little additional flour. Take a clean bowl and brush it lightly with a little more oil, then transfer the dough to the bowl, cover with a clean cloth and leave in a warm place for 30 minutes.

Brush a 900g/2lb loaf tin with a little more oil, roll the dough into an oblong shape and put it into the loaf tin. Cover with a clean cloth and leave in a warm place for a further 30 minutes.

Preheat your oven to 200°C/180°C Fan/Gas Mark 6/400°F.

Brush the top of the loaf with the melted butter. Bake in the centre of the oven for 30 minutes until golden and risen.

Once baked, remove from oven and leave the loaf to cool slightly in tin. Then, turn the loaf out onto a wire rack to cool a little more, before slicing thickly and serving warm.

RYE SOURDOUGH

I usually try to keep a sourdough starter alive, but sometimes life gets in the way. You can ask your local bakery for a small jar. Otherwise, take a look at my starter recipe in Baking Basics, on page 30. This is the only loaf that requires a starter. If you'd like an easier recipe, try the honey and rye loaf from my previous book, *Wild Honey and Rye*, or any of the other breads in this chapter. You can bake this loaf in a Dutch oven (or a large, cast-iron pot with a lid) to help it keep a nice shape.

Makes 1 loaf

For the starter:

50g Sourdough Starter (see Baking Basics, page 30)

150g strong white bread flour

150ml lukewarm water

To finish:

600g strong white bread flour, plus a little extra for dusting

180g dark rye flour

200ml buttermilk or natural yogurt

200ml lukewarm water

20g runny honey

a good pinch of salt

The night before baking, combine the starter ingredients in a jar. Mix well, cover loosely and leave overnight in a warm place.

The next day, in the bowl of a stand mixer fitted with a dough hook, combine the strong white bread flour and the rye flour with the starter mixture. Mix together the buttermilk or yogurt, lukewarm water and honey, then pour in. Mix or knead until a dough forms – it will be quite wet. Cover the bowl with a cloth and set aside in a warm place for 45 minutes.

Sprinkle the salt into the dough mixture and, if the dough is still quite wet, add an extra 2 tablespoons of strong white bread flour, and knead again for a further 5 minutes. Cover and leave to rest in a warm place for a further 30 minutes.

After this time, sprinkle a little flour onto a clean board and knead the dough for 5 minutes by hand (stretch the dough, then use your palm to press down and repeat this a number of times). Cover the dough on the board again and leave in a warm place for 3–4 hours.

Preheat your oven to 240°C/220°C Fan/Gas Mark 9/475°F.

Take some baking paper and scrunch it up, then use it to line your 4 quart Dutch oven or 3.78 litre cast-iron pot. Form the dough into a ball and place it on the baking paper inside the pot. Gently score the top of the bread, then cover with the lid and bake in the oven for 15–20 minutes.

Once baked, transfer the bread onto a wire rack and leave to cool for at least 1 hour before eating.

WILD BLUEBERRY AND ALMOND BABKA LOAF

The *babka* seemed to have something of a resurgence over lockdown and, of course, it is a well-known staple treat within New York delis. The original recipe is said to have originated in the Jewish communities of Poland and Ukraine. This type of *babka* (a sweet braided bread, as opposed to a fluted bundt) was likely taken by the diaspora to Israel, and beyond, establishing itself as a 'yeast cake filled with chocolate, cinnamon and sometimes fruit'. I was interested to learn that in the early 19th century, challah dough was rolled up with jam and baked as a loaf and that the addition of chocolate and other spices was a much later incarnation. Some say the word *babka* comes from the Yiddish *bubbe*, also meaning 'grandmother'. A *babka* made in this way, of twisted strands of dough baked in a loaf form, is different to my earlier recipes for a more cake-like *babka*, baked in a bundt tin and reminiscent of a grandmother's skirt. Rather than using chocolate, I like to make mine with either a home-made preserve or, in this case, with a wild blueberry preserve. There are Polish and French versions of such a preserve in most supermarkets. Ground almonds add a little additional texture and another layer of flavour, but you could use finely chopped hazelnuts, instead. Poppy seed paste also makes a good alternative filling to jam.

Makes 1 loaf

350g plain flour, plus extra for dusting

14g fresh yeast, crumbled (or 7g active dry yeast)

75g caster sugar

75ml lukewarm milk

2 eggs, plus 1 egg yolk, beaten (save the egg white for the glaze)

1 tsp almond extract

grated zest of 1 orange

½ tsp salt

75g butter, cubed, at room temperature

a little sunflower oil, for greasing

For the filling:

300g wild blueberry preserve or any jam of your choice

50g ground almonds

50g soft light brown sugar

For the streusel:

25g cold butter

40g plain flour

25g caster sugar or soft light brown sugar

continued over-leaf

In a jug, combine 1 tablespoon of the flour with the yeast, 1 tablespoon of the caster sugar and half of the lukewarm milk. Stir with a whisk, then set aside in a warm place for 10–15 minutes.

In the bowl of a stand mixer, combine the remaining flour with the rest of the caster sugar and mix well. Pour in the yeast mixture and keep mixing. Switch to a dough hook and add the eggs and egg yolk, the rest of the milk, the almond extract and orange zest, and mix well for around 5 minutes. Finally, add the salt, followed by the butter and keep mixing/kneading for at least 10 minutes. It should form a lump of dough. You will need to stop the mixer and scrape down the sides of the bowl a couple of times. If the dough is still sticky at this point, add up to 2 tablespoons of extra flour.

Brush the inside of a clean bowl with a little oil. Transfer the dough to this bowl and cover with a clean cloth. Leave somewhere warm for at least 2 hours, but ideally 4 hours.

When you are ready to bake, line a loaf tin, measuring 30 x 11 x 7cm/12 x 4¼ x 2¾in, with a single sheet of baking paper, so that a little hangs over the long edges.

Tip the dough out onto a board sprinkled with a generous amount of flour. Punch the dough to get rid of any air pockets and knead for a couple of minutes. Roll out the dough to a 30 x 20cm/12 x 8in rectangle. Spread the preserve/jam for the filling all over the dough, leaving a couple of centimetres

clear around the edge, then sprinkle over the ground almonds and the brown sugar. Roll the dough into a log, starting from one of the longest edges. Take a sharp knife and cut down the centre of the log, dividing the whole length. You will then have two long pieces and be able to see the filling on the inside.

Starting at the top, join the two pieces of dough, then cross them over each other. Keep going, as though you are making a braid. You can trim both ends to neaten them up. Carefully transfer the whole piece of twisted dough into the lined loaf tin. Cover with a clean cloth and chill in the refrigerator for up to 2 hours.

Meanwhile, make the streusel topping. Place all the ingredients in a bowl and rub them together with your fingers until the mixture resembles a crumble or a sandy texture.

Preheat your oven to 180°C/160°C Fan/Gas Mark 4/350°F.

Brush the top of your loaf with the lightly beaten egg white, then sprinkle over the streusel topping. Bake in the centre of the oven for 50 minutes, checking after 35 minutes to see whether the top looks golden. Once it is golden, cover with foil and continue baking for the remaining time. Remove from the oven and leave the *babka* to cool in the tin.

Serve warm, with a little unsalted butter.

POLISH-FRENCH TOAST WITH ROASTED PLUMS

This is a little treat I had at the breakfast markets in Warsaw one sunny summer morning. The breakfast markets are a lovely treat. You meander around various food stalls, which offer everything from baked goods to home-made preserves, Polish honey, freshly baked bread and pickles. There were pancakes served with fruit compote and vegan brownies made with beans and fresh coffee, but the highlight on that morning was a kind of French toast, or *tosty Francuskie*, made with Polish brioche, or *chalka*, also known as *challah*, served with soft and syrupy Polish plums. This is also a great recipe to make if you've got any leftover Wild Blueberry and Almond *Babka* Loaf from page 156.

Serves 4

2 eggs
100ml milk
50ml double cream
1 tsp ground cinnamon
2 tbsp butter, at room temperature
2–3 tbsp vegetable oil
8 medium slices of challah bread
(or use leftover **Babka** *Loaf, page 156)*

For the roasted plums:

4 plums, halved and stoned
3 tbsp soft light brown sugar
a generous drizzle of runny honey

To serve:

100g cream cheese or twaróg sernikowy *(see page 20) (optional)*
2 tbsp icing sugar, optional

Start with the roasted plums. Preheat your oven to 200°C/180°C Fan/Gas Mark 6/400°F.

Place the plums on a baking tray, sprinkle over the sugar and drizzle with honey. Roast in the oven for 30–40 minutes, or until soft. Remove and set aside.

Crack the eggs into a bowl and whisk, then add the milk, cream, cinnamon and 1 teaspoon of the butter. Whisk again until well combined.

Heat a little of the oil and a little of the remaining butter in a frying pan over a medium heat. Dip two slices of the challah or bread into the egg mixture until well coated, then fry for 2–3 minutes on each side, or until golden. Set aside on a plate to keep warm. Repeat with the rest of the bread slices and egg mixture, adding a little oil and butter to the pan each time.

Place two slices of the cooked bread on each plate and top with two roasted plum halves. I like to serve mine with a spoonful of cream cheese and sprinkled generously with icing sugar.

CARROT AND APPLE LOAF CAKE WITH FUDGE DRIZZLE

In Poland, carrot cake is called *ciasto marchewkowe,* and it makes sense in a country where lots of people traditionally had a vegetable garden, or a *działka*. Apples can be found in abundance, too, and this cake, with grated apples, is a firm favourite in our house. The fudge drizzle, or *polewa krówkowa*, can be made with Polish cream fudge called *krówki*, which means 'little cows', or with any soft toffee or fudge sweets. At a push, simply warm a little caramel sauce from a jar.

Serves 8

For the cake:

175g butter, at room temperature, plus a little extra for greasing

175g soft light brown sugar

2 eggs

250g self-raising flour

1 tsp ground cinnamon

1 tsp baking powder

2 carrots, peeled and grated

2 small eating apples, peeled, cored and grated

1 tbsp sour cream or natural yogurt

For the fudge drizzle:

15 fudge sweets, such as krówki, or any soft toffee or fudge sweets

100ml milk

Preheat your oven to 180°C/160°C Fan/Gas Mark 4/350°F. Grease and line a 1kg/2lb/4oz loaf tin with baking paper.

In a food processor or a stand mixer, beat the butter with the brown sugar until pale and creamy. Add the eggs, one by one. Sift in the flour, ground cinnamon and baking powder, and stir until the flour is fully incorporated. Stir in the grated carrots and apples, along with the sour cream or yogurt. Don't overmix.

Pour the mixture into the lined tin and bake on the middle shelf of the oven for 50 minutes. Remove and cover with foil, then bake for a further 10 minutes, or until a skewer inserted into the centre of the cake comes out clean. Leave to cool in the tin, before turning out onto a wire rack or a plate.

For the fudge drizzle, gently heat the fudge sweets with the milk in a small pan, stirring until the fudge melts and you have a thick sauce. Leave to cool a little before drizzling the sauce over the top of the loaf cake, then serve.

DESSERTS, SWEETS, PRESERVES (AND A ŁIQUEUR)

MAMA'S BROWN SUGAR SEMOLINA WITH APPLES AND HONEY OR JAM SAUCE

Semolina pudding always strikes me as something quite old-fashioned, but it's one of the most comforting puddings I know, and was a staple in my house growing up. Mama used to make it for us, sweetened with honey, and sometimes with a sprinkle of brown sugar and some stewed apples. I realise now that it is something she would have eaten a lot growing up in her post-war Polish Resettlement Camp, in Doddington, Cheshire. They lived in barracks, with no heating, and had a communal cookhouse and dining room for the camp's residents, staffed with Polish cooks. The camp's post-war menu shows items such as 'semolina', or 'rice pudding with jam sauce'. It wasn't until the early 1950s that the camps began converting to self-catering facilities, and my grandmother would then get ration stamps to feed the family, saving up or swapping rations for extra milk, sugar and yeast to bake with. To this day, Mama will always have semolina in her larder. In Polish kitchens, it is called *kasza manna*.

Serves 4

For the semolina pudding:

750ml milk

100g soft light brown sugar

1 tsp vanilla bean paste

25g butter

90g semolina

For the jam sauce (optional):

150g jam of your choice

1–2 tbsp water

For the apples and honey (optional):

1 x quantity of Stewed Apples (see Baking Basics, page 25), warmed

a drizzle of runny honey

In a pan, gently bring the milk, brown sugar, vanilla and butter to a rolling boil. Pour in the semolina and stir continuously until the mixture thickens. This will take at least 10 minutes over a low heat. Take care so that the mixture in the bottom of the pan does not burn. Remove from the heat, cover and keep warm.

To make the optional jam sauce, place the jam in a saucepan and heat gently, adding 1–2 tablespoons of water and stirring until you have a sauce consistency.

Serve the semolina pudding with either the jam sauce or a few spoonfuls of warmed stewed apples, drizzled with honey and sprinkled with ground cinnamon.

ELENA'S LAYERED BANANA DESSERT

My daughter Elena loves making these for a family treat at the weekend. It is a very simple *deser bananowy*. If you top it with caramel, it becomes a *bananowa krówka*, for those times when you want a quick sweet hit without too much hard work. You can make these simple desserts in glasses and keep them in the refrigerator in advance of serving them.

Serves 6

150g rich tea biscuits, herbatniki or shortbread cookies

50g butter, melted

4 ripe bananas

300ml double cream or whipping cream

250g cream cheese or twaróg sernikowy (see page 20)

3 tbsp soft light brown sugar

1 tsp vanilla bean extract

50g good-quality dark or milk chocolate and/or Caramel Sauce (see Baking Basics, page 28)

In a food processor, whizz up the biscuits until you have a sandy texture. Tip into a bowl, pour in the melted butter and mix. Divide this mixture among six glass tumblers. Slice two of the bananas and divide them among the glasses on top of the biscuit crumbs.

Whip the double or whipping cream until just thick but still soft, then add the cream cheese, sugar and vanilla, and whisk until incorporated. Divide this evenly among the glasses over the sliced banana.

Slice the remaining two bananas and layer on top of the cream mixture. Drizzle over a little caramel sauce over the bananas and/or grate the dark or milk chocolate on top.

KRÓWKI

Polish Cream Fudge

Krówki, meaning 'little cows', are little Polish cream fudge sweets. I ate them all throughout my childhood. I remember them being wrapped in white and yellow paper, and the sweet fudge had an almost liquid, slightly gooey centre, which is quite hard to replicate when making them at home. Still, this is a nice project, and I like to make a batch and give them away as gifts, in little jars, tied with yellow ribbon.

Makes 30 pieces

1 x 397g can of condensed milk
80g butter
150g soft dark brown sugar
1 tsp vanilla bean paste

Line a 20 x 20cm/8 x 8in square baking tin with baking paper.

Combine the condensed milk, butter, soft brown sugar and vanilla in a wide, non-stick pan and stir over a medium heat with a wooden spoon until the sugar dissolves, making sure it doesn't catch. Once melted, bring the mixture to a rolling boil. Take care, because the mixture will be extremely hot. Stir it constantly for around 10 minutes. If you have a sugar thermometer, the mixture should reach 113°C/235°F. Have a glass of cold water ready and test the fudge by dropping a small amount of the mixture into the cold water. You are looking for the fudge to drop to the bottom of the glass and form a tear shape or ball.

When it's ready, remove the pan from the heat and leave it to cool for a few minutes. Then, using the wooden spoon, stir the mixture vigorously until it begins to firm up a little, about 5 minutes.

Pour the mixture into your lined tin and tap it on the work surface to settle any bubbles. Leave to cool at room temperature for a couple of hours.

Turn out of the tin as one large square onto a board. Chop into rectangular pieces using a sharp knife and wrap each piece in food-safe white and yellow tissue paper to form little *krówki*-inspired sweets.

BUTTER-ROASTED PEARS WITH CHEESECAKE ICE CREAM

This *lody sernikowe*, or cheesecake ice cream, is a 'no-churn' recipe and is so simple to make. It goes so well with roasted fruit, but you can also serve it on its own, or with any dessert of your choice. In her book, *Cook, Eat, Repeat*, Nigella Lawson has a version of cheesecake ice cream, adding lemon and lime juice and advocaat to her cream and condensed milk. I include a recipe for Polish *Adwokat* on page 178, so you could experiment with different variations of this home-made ice cream to serve with your roasted fruit or summer berries. The butter-roasted pears here could be substituted for the Honey-Roasted Plums on page 130.

Serves 4, with ice cream left over

For the cheesecake ice cream:

500g cream cheese or twaróg sernikowy *(see page 20), at room temperature*

1 x 397g can of condensed milk

300ml double cream or whipping cream

For the roasted pears:

2 tbsp butter

4 ripe pears, peeled, halved and cored

125g soft light brown sugar

1 tsp ground cinnamon

1–2 tbsp warm water

To make the ice cream, put the cream cheese into the bowl of a stand mixer and beat well, then add the condensed milk and cream, and whisk until completely smooth and thick. Pour the ice cream mixture into a container with a lid (or I use a 1.3kg/3lb loaf tin lined with clingfilm) and freeze for at least 5 hours, until firm.

For the roasted pears, preheat your oven to 200°C/180°C Fan/Gas Mark 6/400°F.

Melt the butter over a low heat in an ovenproof pan, such as a cast-iron frying pan. Place the pears, cut-side down, into the pan and cook for 15–20 minutes. Sprinkle over the brown sugar and cinnamon and allow the pears to start to caramelise. Flip the pears over, then add the warm water to the pan, so that a syrup forms. Transfer to the oven and bake, uncovered, for 15–20 minutes until the pears are soft. Remove from the oven and cool a little before serving.

Serve the pears warm, with the cheesecake ice cream.

Desserts, Sweets, Preserves (and a Liqueur)

SESAME SNAP POSSETS

GF

Last summer, I ran a Polish supper club at Ognisko Polskie, the Polish Hearth Club, in London, with my friend James Lewis – a former lawyer and a chef who, like me, is deeply proud of his Polish heritage. We settled on a sharing supper, which was a huge and memorable feast, assisted by Jan Woroniecki and his team in the kitchen. For dessert, we served a selection of mini desserts, including my apple *szarlotka*, pancake fritters (*racuchy*), and cheesecake squares. James made tahini possets, echoing the flavours of a sesame snap biscuit (*sezamki*), which he and I both used to eat as kids. They were a big hit, so I've tried to recreate them here. Since sesame snaps are gluten-free, I use arrowroot to help thicken the dessert, which makes this an easy gluten-free dessert.

Makes 8

1 tsp ground arrowroot

1 tbsp water

100g tahini or sesame paste

500ml double cream

200g soft light brown sugar

4 x 30g sesame snap biscuit packets or *sezamki* (12 sesame snaps in total)

Mix the arrowroot with the water to form a paste. Mix the jar of tahini or sesame paste well, as there will be a little oil on the top, before measuring it out.

Put the double cream and sugar in a pan and gently bring to the boil, then add the arrowroot paste and tahini, whisking it all together well. Stir the mixture until the sugar has dissolved and then heat for 3–4 minutes until bubbles start to come to the surface. Remove from the heat and leave to cool slightly.

Stir again and then divide the mixture between eight small ramekins or dessert pots. I usually use a funnel to pour it in, as it is less messy. Refrigerate overnight, uncovered.

The next day, whizz four of the sesame snap biscuits into very fine crumbs in a food processor. Sprinkle the crumbs over the possets and serve each one with an individual sesame snap on the side.

ŚLIWKI W CZEKOLADZIE

Plums Coated in Chocolate

Śliwki w czekoladzie are another classic Polish sweet treat. I usually get packets of them every Christmas and then they sit in my cupboard for months. However, there is something quite comforting about them, and if you make them yourself at home, you can experiment with fair-trade chocolate, or a good-quality chocolate of your choice. The plum inside is a soft stoned dried prune, so make sure you buy the pitted variety. They don't really work with prunes in syrup, because the chocolate slips off, but you can make a 'cheeky' version by soaking your prunes in a little vodka first (obviously, don't give these to your children!).

Makes 12

24 soft dried prunes such as Agen, stoned

2–3 tbsp vodka (optional)

150g good-quality dark chocolate (or experiment with milk chocolate, or vegan chocolate)

dried rose petals or dried blue cornflowers, to decorate

If using, soak the prunes in vodka overnight. When you are ready to use them, put them on a few sheets of kitchen paper to dry them off.

Set a large, heatproof bowl over a pan of simmering water (making sure the bottom of the bowl doesn't touch the water) and break the chocolate into pieces in the bowl. Melt over a very low heat, only stirring occasionally once melted. Remove from the heat. Take two stoned prunes and squash them together to make them stick into one larger piece, then carefully dip into the melted chocolate until completely coated. Use a spoon to take each coated prune out and place on a sheet of baking paper.

To make them look pretty, sprinkle over some dried rose petals or dried (crushed) cornflowers while the chocolate is still a little warm. Leave them to cool before eating, so that the chocolate sets around each prune.

QUINCE OR APRICOT JAM WITH TEA

I've included this recipe for quince jam, as I often see quinces in season at my local Italian delicatessen and never know what to do with them. However, you can also use apricots instead of quinces. In Poland, quince jam is quite popular and you can use this recipe for any of the layer cakes in this book. It is also lovely with the pancakes on page 128 in place of the apricot jam. Quince fruit is called *pigwa*, which is one of my favourite Polish words. The Poles also often drink *herbata z konfiturą*, or tea with jam, and this quince jam is perfect for that as a winter warmer. Whenever I drink tea with jam, I always think of my good friend Krystyna Małkowska-Żaba, granddaughter of the founders of Polish Scouting, as she drinks tea with jam, especially in the winter when she visits snowy Zakopane, where there is a museum dedicated to her grandparents. I am also very proud of my connections to Polish scouting, and have a wonderful group of friends in our circle, Krąg Starszoharcerski 'Zawisza'. We love reminiscing and singing Polish scouting songs, made all the better with a cup of tea, *herbatka*.

Makes 2 jars

For the quince jam:

1kg quince

500g jam sugar

1 tsp lemon juice

1-2 tbsp water

For the tea:

1 pot of freshly brewed tea

1 tsp quince or apricot jam (or use any jam of your choice)

½ tsp ground cinnamon (optional)

1 slice of orange or lemon

To make the jam, wash and dry the quince, slice in half and remove any pips, then cube. Put the quince cubes in a large bowl, add the sugar and lemon juice and mix. Cover and leave in the refrigerator for 1 hour. The quince should start to release some juices.

Place a side plate in the freezer, ready for testing the jam later.

Tip the rested quince into a large pan, add the water and bring to a gentle boil. Turn up the heat and boil gently for a further 30 minutes, removing any foam that forms on the top. If you have a sugar thermometer, the jam should reach 105°C/221°F. You can also test your jam by placing a teaspoon of it onto your chilled plate. Leave it for a minute or two. The jam should be quite thick and when you push your finger through it, it should wrinkle. If it is not setting, keep boiling it for a few more minutes, then repeat the chilled plate test.

Once the jam is ready, transfer it to sterilised jars and seal. It will keep for 2–3 months in a cool, dark place. Once opened, the jam can be stored in a refrigerator for up to one month.

For the tea with jam, brew a pot of tea. Stir in the jam, the cinnamon and the pared zest, then pour into cups to serve.

For the apricot jam version, boil gently for 20 minutes.

Desserts, Sweets, Preserves (and a Liqueur)

BLUEBERRY JAM

This is a very easy jam to make. In season, I always make it with blueberries, or with wild bilberries in Poland. Blackcurrants work well, too, which always reminds me of the blackcurrant bush we had in our garden growing up. You can use this for the *Babka* Loaf recipe on page 156, or to fill the Polish Doughnuts on page 90.

Makes 2 jars

700g blueberries, bilberries or blackcurrants

350g caster sugar or granulated sugar

2 tsp lemon juice

1 tsp vanilla bean paste

Wash the berries or blackcurrants well and tip them into a bowl. Add the sugar, lemon juice and vanilla bean paste and mix well. Leave to stand for 30 minutes or so.

Place a side plate in the freezer, ready for testing the jam later.

Tip the fruit into a large, heavy-based pan and bring to the boil. Let it boil gently for 10 minutes, removing any foam that forms on the top. If you have a sugar thermometer, the jam should reach 105°C/221°F. You can also test your jam by placing a teaspoon of it onto your chilled plate. Leave it for a minute or two. The jam should be quite thick and when you push your finger through it, it should wrinkle. If it is not setting, keep boiling it for a few more minutes, then repeat the chilled plate test.

Once the jam is ready, leave it to cool completely then transfer it to sterilised jars and seal. It will keep for 2–3 months in a cool, dark place. Once opened, the jam can be stored in a refrigerator for up to one month.

Desserts, Sweets, Preserves (and a Liqueur)

ADWOKAT

Advocaat Liqueur

I couldn't leave this sweet Polish cookbook without giving you a recipe for a sweet tipple. If cocktails or flavoured vodkas are your thing, then I would refer you to chapter 7 of my previous book, *Wild Honey and Rye*, which features an abundance of fruit liqueurs and flavoured vodkas called *nalewki*. I mentioned this liqueur in my earlier recipe for Doughnuts with Custard or Advocaat Cream (page 86), and while you can easily buy this liqueur, it does make for a lovely home-based project, particularly in winter. Advocaat is a Dutch liqueur made with eggs, sugar and brandy, but as mentioned earlier, the Poles make their own version with vodka. It is sometimes called *ajerkoniak* (*ajer* from *eier*, meaning 'egg', and *koniak* meaning 'cognac' in Dutch). It likely came to Poland with Dutch advocates practising law. Once cooled, you can rewarm it gently and serve it with cream on top (see *Bombardino*, page 180), or use it for an eggnog-style cocktail.

Makes 2 x 500ml bottles

6 egg yolks

250g caster sugar

1 tsp vanilla bean paste

1 x 397g can of condensed milk or 300ml double cream

250ml good-quality 40%-proof vodka (you can also make it with brandy)

Place a large, heatproof bowl over a pan of simmering water (making sure the bottom of the bowl doesn't touch the water). Add the egg yolks, sugar and vanilla, and whisk over a very gentle heat. Add half of the condensed milk or cream and stir for 5 minutes. The sugar should have dissolved.

Remove the mixture from the heat and stir in the remaining condensed milk or cream. Finally, slowly pour in the vodka and mix well. Leave to cool, then pour into sterilised bottles and seal.

Chill in the refrigerator for at least 24 hours. The mixture will thicken. Store in the refrigerator until you are ready to drink it, or use it as a doughnut filling mixed with custard. Use within three months, and keep it stored in the refrigerator.

BOMBARDINO

This is a classic Italian drink, but I had it once in the ski resort of Białka Tatrzańska in Poland. This is one of my sister Wanda's favourite drinks over the festive season. Scale up as necessary!

Makes 1

25ml **Adwokat** *(see page 178) or advocaat*

25ml *brandy*

50ml *whipping or double cream, whipped*

a sprinkle of ground cinnamon

In a small, heatproof bowl over a small pan of gently simmering water (making sure the bowl doesn't touch the water), very gently heat the *adwokat* or advocaat liqueur along with the brandy until warm.

Pour into a heatproof glass and top with the whipped cream and a sprinkling of cinnamon. Warning – this packs a punch!

RESOURCES

FOR POLISH FOOD IN LONDON:
- Ognisko Restaurant, 55 Exhibition Road, London SW7 2PG (Ground floor of the Polish Hearth Club, non-member are welcome in the restaurant)
- Daquise Restaurant, 20 Thurloe St, South Kensington, London SW7 2LT
- Sowa Patisserie 32-33 High Street, Ealing Broadway

FOR POLISH FOOD IN MANCHESTER:
- Plazki Restaurant, 229 Deansgate, Manchester M3 4EN
- Barbakan Deli, 67-71 Manchester Rd, Chorlton-cum-Hardy, Manchester M21 9PW

POLISH ARTISAN PRODUCTS ONLINE WITH UK NATIONWIDE DELIVERY:
- https://www.mymaja.co.uk/en/
- Polish-family owned honey company, made in Scotland: http://www.edinburghhoney.co.uk/
- Fruit vinegar and live vinegar made in Poland. https://www.en.octovnia.pl/

POLISH EVENTS IN LONDON:
- https://instytutpolski.pl/london/

INTERESTING ARTICLES ABOUT POLISH FOOD:
- https://culture.pl/en/search/food

INDEX

ACKNOWLEDGEMENTS

*"Writing means sharing. It's part of the human condition
to want to share things – thoughts, ideas, opinions."* – Paulo Coelho

While it is generally my approach to life to get things done, this book has come about quietly, over time. I have had great fun baking, creating, testing and tweaking. This book has involved research and travel and reminiscing and sharing. It has been punctuated by life events, and it has woven itself seamlessly around the strands of a busy family life and work life. Sometimes, the best projects are those that do become part of the fabric of our lives, and they come about in their own time.

When writing my first book, *Wild Honey and Rye*, I had in mind my second book would have a sweet theme and the tiny seed planted back then has grown into something so very special now. It was with great joy, and good fortune, that my proposal for *The Sweet Polish Kitchen* came to be commissioned by my publishers Pavilion Books as they found a new home at HarperCollins. To this end, I must first thank my literary agent Heather Holden-Brown for her unfailing positivity and for continuing to have steadfast faith in me, along with Elly James at HHB Agency who has also been so very encouraging. A special thank you also to Cara Armstrong who sensed "charm and atmosphere" when this book was just an idea and who carried it forward in its infancy.

Onwards, this book was supported by Lisa Milton, Executive Publisher at HarperCollins. Thank you to Lisa for welcoming me into the Pavilion HarperCollins family. My thanks also to Stephanie Milner, who, having edited my first book, happened upon me again as she became Publishing Director at Pavilion Books. Managing Editor Clare Double steered the project with plenty of positivity, patience and collaboration, for which I am truly thankful. *The Sweet Polish Kitchen* then gracefully moved into the editing sphere of Ellen Simmons, who has continued to keep a close eye on the detail to the finish line. Thank you to Emily Preece-Morrison, who I had also worked with during my first book, for her attention to detail through her copy editing.

Onto the shoots. As I stepped into Nassima Rothacker's studio for the first time, I breathed in the aromas of healing oils and candles, and Nassima's calming herbal tea blends. I was immediately transported to a place of ethereal energy. The photographs in this book are as beautiful as they are because they were taken by such an amazing human. I will forever be grateful to Nassima, for the care, attention and creativity that she brought to the pages of this book. Thank you also for the delicious lunches we were treated to on set (to balance out the cake) and to the photography assistants, Kee, Charlotte and Eyder, who looked after us, too.

Bringing together wondrous creative magic was Joss Herd, a food styling legend and one of the best in the business. Joss was simply a joy to work with. I was (and am) in awe of her ability to breathe life into a few simple words on a page, understanding how a recipe needs to come together, planning and sourcing with precision. Thank you to Hattie Baker, assistant food stylist, for bringing to the table her expertise in shaping, rising, rolling and filling, and who, like Joss, was never phased by the task in hand. I am indebted to Tabitha

Hawkins, too, who sourced the most beautiful, thoughtful props and who very kindly incorporated some of my special Polish family linens and extra *accoutrements* as the recipes were transposed from the kitchen to Nassima's lens.

The design of this book is down to the acutely talented Laura Russell and her team. It has been an absolute joy to work with Laura across both books, and I am so grateful for her unique vision and for interpreting and embracing 'Polish nostalgia' with such creativity.

My thanks to the domestic and international sales team at Pavilion HarperCollins and to Komal Patel and her marketing team for giving this book the chance to soar as it flew the nest. Thank you to Michel Moushabeck at Interlink Books in America for his continued support of my writing and for his early endorsement of *The Sweet Polish Kitchen* – even before seeing the full spreads.

Behind the scenes, I have to thank my Mama, Alicja Marczak, because without her, my own sense of identity would never have been so deeply ingrained. And to my father, who has passed, but who instilled within me a great sense that Poland was never just a place on a map. Actually, Dad was obsessed with maps and with Poland's historical border shifts throughout the ages. It seemed odd to me growing up, but now I understand. His feet, as a young man, planted so firmly in Polish soil. That soil, and those borders, so vulnerable to shifting.

Thank you to my husband, Ed, for his continued faith in me and for his unfading support. A big thank you also to my daughter, Elena, for her help with recipe testing, weighing and measuring, and to my sons Edward and Matthew for being ever-present cake testers, along with my mum-in-law Kathy, whose feedback was always wholly positive. To my sisters Elizabeth, Wanda and Basia and brother Roman, for holding everything together during challenging times. To my closest friends in Sale and to my NCT ladies in St Albans for the encouraging chats, often over cake, or fizz, or both. And to Anna Wilk, for her support, and Polish honey. I would also like to thank Gillian Marczak, my godmother, who as a home economist and food stylist gave me some valuable feedback during the early stages of recipe development. In Poland, thank you to Urszula Gacek of Octovnia, and her son Marek, for driving Monika and I around Polish country lanes and painted villages. And to Monika's sister Ewa, for sending me the very special *Katarzynki* cookie cutters.

As much as I set out to celebrate the sweet side of Polish cooking, honouring my Polish roots along the way, I have ended up doing so much more than this. *The Sweet Polish Kitchen* brings together my upbringing and heritage, and evokes so many memories, whether my own, or for others whose memories may have faded. This process has been deeply soothing as well as healing and many people have inspired me through the adventure. To write *is* to share, and I am so fortunate to be able to share these recipes with you all.

Finally, to all who will go on to buy, bake from and support this book – thank you.

Smacznego i dziękuję serdecznie za wsparcie.

Renatka x

Rogal Marciński
6 zł szt

Pavilion
An imprint of HarperCollinsPublishers Ltd
1 London Bridge Street
London SE1 9GF

www.harpercollins.co.uk

HarperCollinsPublishers
1st Floor, Watermarque Building
Ringsend Road Dublin 4
Ireland

10 9 8 7 6 5 4 3 2 1

First published in Great Britain by
Pavilion, an imprint of HarperCollinsPublishers Ltd
2024

Copyright © Ren Behan 2024

Ren Behan asserts the moral right to be identified
as the author of this work. A catalogue record for
this book is available from the British Library.

ISBN 978-0-00-859010-9

FSC™ MIX
Paper | Supporting responsible forestry
FSC™ C007454
www.fsc.org

This book is produced from independently
certified FSC™ paper to ensure responsible
forest management.

For more information visit:
www.harpercollins.co.uk/green

Printed and bound in Malaysia

Publishing Director: Stephanie Milner
Managing Editor: Clare Double
Assistant Editor: Ellen Simmons
Design Director: Laura Russell
Designer: James Boast
Illustrator: Nelly Edwards
Copy editor: Emily Preece-Morrison
Proofreader: Anne Sheasby
Production controller: Grace O'Byrne
Cover concept: Maeve Bargman

WHEN USING KITCHEN APPLIANCES PLEASE
ALWAYS FOLLOW THE MANUFACTURER'S
INSTRUCTIONS